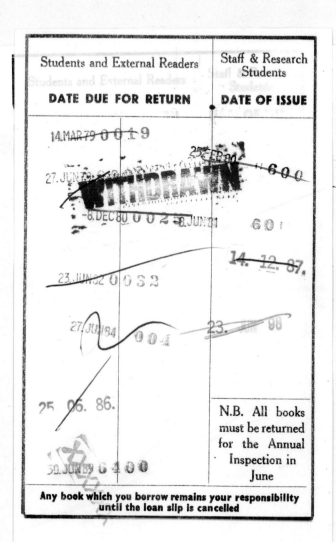

Students and External Readers | Staff & Research Students

DATE DUE FOR RETURN | **DATE OF ISSUE**

14. MAR 79 0 0 1 9

27. JUN   25 FEB 80   600

WITHDRAWN

-8. DEC 80 0 0 2 8. JUN 81   601

14. 12. 87.

23. JUN 82 0 0 3 2

27. JUN 84 004   23. JUN 88

25 06. 86.

N.B. All books must be returned for the Annual Inspection in June

30. JUN 89 0 4 0 0

Any book which you borrow remains your responsibility until the loan slip is cancelled

Sharing Inflation?

POVERTY REPORT 1976

A report of
the Institute of
Community
Studies

TEMPLE SMITH
London

Poverty Report 1976

SHARING INFLATION?

Edited by
PETER WILLMOTT

First published in Great Britain 1976
by Maurice Temple Smith Ltd
37 Great Russell Street, London WC1
© 1976 Institute of Community Studies
IBSN 0 85117 1036 cased/0 85117 1028/paperback
Printed in Great Britain by
Billing & Sons Ltd
Guildford and London

Contents

Part 3 Perspectives

1 Introduction

PETER WILLMOTT

When the history of contemporary Britain comes to be written, there is no doubt about the label that will be attached to 1975. It will surely be remembered as the 'year of inflation'. During much of the year the annual rate of price increases exceeded 25%, something that had never happened before in peace time. The shock to the British economy and to British society was great. This book is mainly about the consequences of that shock for the poor.

The fall in the value of money was, of course, not new. Since at least 1945 the cost of living had risen every year, and the housewives' outrage had lost each party more than one general election. But, in the fever of early 1975, the inflation of earlier postwar years seemed relatively gentle. What on earth had people been worrying about before? The new fear was that the steep rise to 25% could easily turn to 50%, 50% to 100%, and then anything might happen. People remembered stories of Germany in the 1920s; the basket stuffed with thousand-mark notes, left unattended for a few minutes, that was stolen – but its contents left behind. If Britain's inflation took anything like that runaway course, the consequences would obviously be disastrous for the economy and for the living standards of virtually everybody.

By the middle of the year anxiety had grown almost to panic, so that in July, when the government published its White Paper, *The Attack on Inflation*, there was general support for the harsh policies it proposed. By the autumn, in unprecedented fashion, the Trades Union Congress (TUC), the Labour Party Conference and, if the opinion polls are to be believed, the majority of the British people were willing to accept the need for tough measures.

Towards the end of the year it looked as if the government's policies were having some effect. The rate of inflation had started to slow down somewhat and it seemed possible that the objective of reducing the annual increase in prices to 10% or less by the end of 1976 might be achieved.

Even if the rate of inflation is successfully checked, that will solve only part of the problem. The nation that started off industrialisation has become 'the sick man of Europe'. Other countries have emulated Britain, bettering the instruction, and the teacher now lies enfeebled. We have of course been hit by world inflation, triggered (as Charles Elliott shows in Chapter 9) largely but not only by the quadrupling of oil prices during 1972 and 1973. Britain's own inflation was particularly steep and tenacious because it was accelerated by the deeper domestic economic crisis – of investment and productivity, of output and unemployment, of exports and the balance of payments, of falling confidence in sterling and consequential devaluation – that has plagued the country and all its governments since 1945. It is this underlying weakness of the economy that made it difficult for Britain to control inflation as successfully as most other countries. It is this that made drastic action necessary.

The government's main measures were, first, the £6 a week earnings limit and, secondly, the cuts in public spending, which were anticipated in the July White Paper but were still being worked out in detail as this book went to press at the end of 1975. The aim of these policies was clear. In 1974, despite the oil cartel, the general standard of living had risen – earnings had gone up faster than prices. This was possible only because we borrowed heavily from abroad. We could not go on doing that, not even by continuing to mortgage North Sea oil. Thus in 1975, if we were to begin to get straight, the general standard of living needed to fall. Because of the government's policies, and the response to them, it did. Our question, of course, is how the poor fared in this process compared with other people.

In trying to answer this question, the emphasis is somewhat different from that of last year's *Poverty Report*. The main question then was how the living standards of the poor had been affected by inflation itself. The question this year, to a much greater extent, is about the effects of the government's policies to check inflation.

If good intentions were enough, the poor would have little to complain of. The government stressed, as a crucial feature of its package, its aim of protecting the worst off. The objective was, in a period of falling living standards, to maintain those of the poorest people. The pamphlet based on the July White Paper argued that the government's programme was 'fair':

> It is fair because everybody, except the lower-paid, is called on to accept some cuts in living standards . . . It is fair because the £6 pay limit means that the lower-paid can get proportionately most, and the best-off will get nothing. It is fair because there are provisions to help the worse-off . . . (*Attack on Inflation*: *A Policy for Survival* 1975).

On the face of it, most of the pledges seem to have been kept. It looks as if the government has so far tried to share out the consequences of its counter-inflation policies in ways that harmed the poor least. The trouble is that some things have not worked out. As the story unfolds in succeeding chapters, it will become evident that, despite hopes to the contrary, many of the poor are worse off and, as the cuts in public spending bite, there will be more suffering.

In the chapters that follow, the two crucial planks of official policy are discussed in turn. Part 1 is mainly about incomes (and to some extent about prices, which determine what incomes can buy). Part 2 concentrates on the cuts in public spending, in the course of reviewing recent trends in major services. I shall explain later the intended contribution of Part 3.

What happened to incomes?

If inflation was to be checked, the government had to have an 'incomes policy' that trade unions and employers would honour. If the low paid were to be protected, a flat-rate limit was a good idea. Hence Jack Jones's proposal, accepted by the TUC and then by the government. For the poor it was without doubt the right formula, and it must be a matter for congratulation that it was taken up and implemented.

What is more, as Chris Trinder concludes in Chapter 2, in December 1975 it seemed to be more or less working in the way intended. Large numbers of low-paid workers were getting the full £6 increase, and this meant, in terms of gross pay at least, substantial improvements in the relative position of many of them in a period of general restraint. As he also shows, however, there were exceptions, particularly among workers in the private sector (the clothing trades, for instance) as against the public. There were still many earning less than the £30 a week recommended as a minimum by the TUC in 1974 and accepted by the government; it is a low enough level, not having been increased since then in line with either prices or average earnings.

Any satisfaction one might draw from the £6 a week policy is diluted by Chapter 3, which looks not just at gross pay but at what low-paid earners actually receive. Mr Jones's excellent proposal would have been more egalitarian in its effect were it not for Mr Healey and his Treasury colleagues. The 1975 Budget increased the tax burden in real terms on low-paid workers, treating them more harshly than the better off. As their money incomes increased, families also lost some rebates and allowances through the operation of the so-called 'poverty trap'. Trinder shows that, when changes in taxes and in eligibility for the various benefits and rebates are taken into account along with price increases, a married couple on low pay and with four children was likely to have had a drop of 9% in its standard of living between October 1974 and October 1975.

With social security benefits, part of the subject matter of Chapter 4, the story is a mixed one. As explained in *Poverty Report 1975*, the government took a major step forward in 1974 when it agreed henceforth to peg benefits for people on the long-term rates, such as pensioners, to increases in prices or earnings, whichever was greater. The decision was welcome, though it would have been even more so if it had included those on short-term scales who were promised increases only in line with prices. The trouble in implementing the idea, as Trinder shows, is that everything depends on the timing of increases and the indices to which they are related. It does not seem so far as if even those on long-term rates are really having their level of income protected against inflation.

What is more, as Chapter 4 also shows, there are other

worries: for instance, the refusal of long-term rates to the unemployed even when they have been off work for several years, and the failure to make any increase at all, in line with inflation, to some benefits such as maternity and death grants. So in terms of income generally, despite any egalitarian euphoria generated by the £6 a week, it cannot be said that the living standards of the poor, whether they are earning or not, have been universally or satisfactorily safeguarded.

What will happen to services?

One of the difficulties in discussing the effects of the cuts in public spending was that, at the end of 1975, they were still largely to come. There was no doubt that some services were already suffering, and that the future economies would be on such a large scale that they would be bound to hurt. If 1975 was inflation year, 1976 will become known as the year – or rather the first year – of massive cuts in services.

Phyllis Willmott, in Chapter 6, shows how difficult it will be for local authorities to judge where to make economies in their welfare services. To decide how to reduce spending without damaging the worst off demands the wisdom of Solomon, as well as a good deal of detailed information (seldom available) about exactly who benefits most from what. The danger, as she argues, is that local authorities, forced to make their decisions in a hurry, may make the wrong ones. Some of the cuts will certainly reduce the standard of living of some deprived people.

Housing is something of an exception. It was explicitly singled out for encouragement in the Queen's Speech in November 1975, in which it was promised that the government would 'take energetic action to encourage the provision of more houses in both public and private sectors'. That pledge will be welcome if it is backed by resources. But, as Chris Holmes shows in Chapter 7, there is more to housing than new construction. Restrictions on council spending have dramatically cut improvement work and, although some improvement grants were misused in the past, the scale of the reduction means, as he says, that it is likely to have 'adversely affected many people in poor living conditions'. Other measures to improve older property have also been trimmed.

As for education, Stella Duncan and Michael Young argue that it is 'on the defensive'; in local authorities' budgets it is

particularly 'vulnerable as the biggest spender' and is bound to
feel the axe. In its own advice to local authorities, the government suggested some damaging cuts. For example, it recommended cuts in teaching staff in areas losing population; but
these are likely to include the deprived inner city areas where
education so needs to be sustained.

Towards fairness

The obvious question is what can be done? It is going to be
virtually impossible, except on a few limited fronts, to ensure
any absolute improvement in the circumstances of the poor in
1976. For the time being, it seems that the best we can hope for
is to maintain the living standards of the poor, even though
general standards continue to fall. To do this would be in line
with the government's professed intentions cited earlier. The
measures must, in the government's own term, be 'fair' and not
just appear to be so.

On wages, the first concern is with the policy to succeed the
£6 a week (assuming this policy still holds by August 1976). In
the interest of the lower paid and of greater income equality,
there is everything to be said for another flat-rate limit. But, as
Mr Healey argued in the Queen's Speech debate and as the
National Institute of Economic and Social Research pointed
out in its quarterly review at the end of 1975, there would be
bound to be strong objections: 'if the follow-up does not allow
progress in the re-establishment of differentials, it will run into
difficulties' (National Institute of Economic and Social
Research 1975). Even if that proves to be so, it is essential for
the new formula to give preferential treatment to the lower
paid.

Two things in particular need to be done. The first is to
ensure that some of the low paid are not left out, as they were in
1975. Everybody below the TUC/government minimum
weekly wage should move up to it; and the £30 figure should
itself be increased to allow for increases in prices. Secondly, as
Trinder proposes, the government should take a closer look at
the effect of income tax and insurance contributions on the low
paid, and ensure that the wage increases given to such families
with one hand are not taken away with the other. As for social
security benefits, they obviously ought to be maintained at
levels, and on terms and conditions, that genuinely protect the

standards of those dependent on them.

Something more could also be done about prices. There are arguments on both sides about the desirability of large-scale spending on food subsidies as a permanent element in policy. But in a time of rapid inflation there is, from the point of view of the poor, a lot to be said for holding food prices down with subsidies, particularly if they are concentrated on foods that loom large in the diet of lower income families. The case for this policy has been forcibly put by the new National Consumer Council (NCC), launched by the government in January 1975. More generally, the NCC has put the interests of poorer consumers high on its agenda, as was shown in *For Richer, For Poorer*, the report presented to its first national congress (National Consumer Council 1975).

As for services, though Phyllis Willmott acknowledges the difficulties faced by local authorities in deciding on their cuts, she argues against the introduction of new – or the reinforcement of old – means tests for the kind of services particularly benefiting poor people or providing the kinds of general support that 'should not be rationed by income but only by medical or social criteria'. Stella Duncan and Michael Young, while putting in a special plea for educationally deprived areas, make a general case for redistribution down the age scale of those in full-time education, as 'a redistribution from those who benefit most to those who benefit least'.

Such pointers as these can be no more than part of a holding operation, an attempt to protect the poor in the months ahead. It is reasonable to demand this on their behalf. The overriding argument is not that they ought not to suffer disproportionately, though, despite the government's intentions, that is exactly what seems to be happening and likely to continue. It is that, given their present disadvantage in an unequal society, they above all should not have to suffer from inflation or the measures against it.

Housing is apparently less threatened than other services. But housing policies, although so crucial (as shown by the Paris-London comparison in Chapter 10), are weakened at present by the contradictions identified by Chris Holmes. He therefore particularly concentrates on the need for a comprehensive strategy for housing. Most of his suggestions could be implemented fairly quickly.

Holmes also argues for a more general 'strategy against poverty'. It is a plea that is echoed by his fellow contributors; most other chapters include some discussion of the longer-term issues. And, though it is right to concentrate on the immediate task of protecting the poor in the difficult period ahead, it is surely also right that we should as a nation be thinking now about the more fundamental issues.

If a crumb of comfort can be drawn from our present travails, it is that the recent debate about fairness and justice has perhaps made more people aware of the inequalities of British society and of the need to do something about them. This is clearly a difficult time to demand ambitious and expensive new measures. But, gloomy though the immediate prospect is, the economy is likely to pick up in time; North Sea oil will flow, the balance of payments improve, industrial output and productivity rise, unemployment fall. We should be laying plans now for what will then be possible: a major onslaught on poverty in all its dimensions.

In terms of the working poor, the aim should be a minimum wage something like two-thirds of average earnings. If this were accepted, success would depend on resisting the automatic demands for differentials to be maintained; the 'ratchet effect' of that would simply give yet another hoist to inflation and leave many of the worst off where they were. What is needed is to reduce differentials right up the scale, so as to 'concertina' the British wage and salary structure, as has already started to happen in a small way under the £6 policy.

We also need a long-term strategy to give income support for children and to those adults who cannot work, for instance because they are retired, unemployed, single parents or disabled. There is more than one way of organising this support. One possibility would be an improved version of the present varied set of arrangements to meet the needs of different sections of the dependent population. Another would be some kind of tax credit system. As long as the levels of payment were high enough, the new child benefit scheme discussed in Chapter 5 could fit in with either of these. Whatever the form of administration, Britain needs a comprehensive income maintenance scheme: (a) providing substantially higher levels than at present; (b) guaranteed at a fixed minimum ratio to average earnings; (c) automatic rather than dependent on means tests; and

(d) related to taxes and other benefits in such a way as to avoid the poverty trap.

Though there will certainly be major difficulties to be resolved, it would be perfectly possible to design such a scheme. It would also be possible to relate it to a comprehensive programme covering housing, health, welfare, education and the other services. If a debate about strategies and methods is launched now, the electorate will be more likely to give its support when the time is ripe. Then, as real incomes rise, people will be ready to forego something of the improvement in their own prosperity so as to narrow the gap, once and for all, between the living standards and life chances of the poor and those of the majority.

The wider scene

So far this introduction, reflecting the concerns that dominate the first two-thirds of the book, has mainly been about pressing problems inside Britain. Part 3 tries to take some wider perspectives.

Charles Elliott, in Chapter 9, raises the same issues on a world scale as do Parts 1 and 2 at a national one. Their question is about the relative circumstances of poor people in one country racked by inflation. His is about the relative circumstances of poor countries – and particularly the poorest people in poor countries – in the context of world inflation. His chapter shows the cruel turn of the screw made by inflation on many of the world's poor. It is also a sharp reminder of the responsibilities Britain should accept towards the developing countries. Our own problems at home are no excuse for failing to play a full part in combating world poverty.

The final chapters of the book are about research. Chapter 10, by Pierre Aiach and myself, continues on a more modest scale the cross-national theme opened by the Anglo-German comparisons in last year's *Poverty Report*. An intensive study of multiple deprivation in a Paris *quartier* is compared with some similar research in Lambeth. The final chapter, by Lucy Syson, is a review of recent poverty research in Britain. Since research needs to play a continuing role in shaping anti-poverty policies, it is valuable to have an assessment of what has been done and what research could usefully contribute in the future.

Finally, thanks are due to the Department of the Environ-

ment for permission to use material from the Lambeth Inner
Area Study in Chapters 6 and 10.

References

Attack on Inflation: A Policy for Survival (1975), HMSO
National Consumer Council (1975) *For Richer, For Poorer: Some Problems of
    Low-Income Consumers*
The Attack on Inflation (1975) Cmnd 6151, HMSO

1 Incomes

The terms of the social contract were radically revised in July 1975. What happened to the wages of the low paid before and after the change? Has any progress been made in improving their lot?

2   The social contract and the low paid

CHRIS TRINDER

The social contract is a centrepiece of the Labour government's policies. In March 1974, the first month of Labour in office, Mr Healey spoke about 'the social contract on which the solutions to all our problems must depend'. In December 1975 both the Trades Union Congress and Mr Wilson were talking about the development of the social contract for the future beyond July 1976. On the wages side, with many workers having settlements once a year and most agreements being negotiated during the winter months, the social contract in large part concerns this annual wages round. For the one August 1974 to July 1975, henceforth called the 1974-75 wages round, pay increases were supposed to have been no more than the rise in the cost of living, with two main exceptions. Those with basic wage rates of less than £30 for a 40-hour week could get more and women could move towards equal pay. In the August 1975 to July 1976 incomes policy, from now on referred to as the 1975-76 wages round, the increase is limited to £6 a week for everyone except those already on £8,500 a year or more who can get nothing extra.

The social contract has implications for the low paid. Official figures released at the end of 1975 showed that 1.8 million adult men and women are still earning less than £30 for a full week's work (Department of Employment 1975a). Where these are sole breadwinners, either as one-parent families or where the wife is at home looking after young children, they are close to the official poverty line.

Family Income Supplement (FIS) was designed to help such families, but it fills only half the gap between low earnings and prescribed income levels. A major official study of the working poor published in 1975 showed that one in eight of all FIS recipients still remained with total household income below the supplementary benefit poverty line (Department of Health and Social Security 1975). Moreover claiming FIS is no simple matter (Atkinson 1975). As a result it is officially estimated that only about half of those eligible receive it. Altogether, of the households with incomes below the supplementary benefit level in December 1974, 130,000 were headed by a person in full-time work. Michael Foot at the 1975 Labour Party Conference argued that the biggest differential was between 'those who have got a job and those who have not', but this should not mask the fact that many people earn poverty wages, with a wide gap between what they get and average earnings.

I should perhaps explain what this chapter is not. My subject is not low pay generally. There is now a Low Pay Unit which focuses specifically on this issue (Low Pay Unit, 9 Poland Street, London W1); via bi-monthly low pay bulletins and papers and pamphlets, it has during 1975 given a clearer picture than has ever existed before of low pay in Britain. Also I am not particularly concerned here with longer term policies. The Employment Protection Bill, a major piece of legislation, was enacted in 1975 and in the future may have substantial implications for the low paid. The Low Pay Unit, which itself tried to get certain provisions inserted into the Bill, published briefing notes on this too (Low Pay Unit 1975a).

In this chapter and the next I look at the actual effects of recent government pay policy on the worst off. I concentrate here on gross pay and in the next chapter I take account of deductions such as income tax and national insurance contributions, additions like family allowances and rent and rate rebates, and inflation. The analysis concentrates throughout on the position of those with the lowest earnings, but they are – as they clearly must be – examined in relation to the rest of the population.

In the first section of this chapter, using data from the government's annual earnings survey, I look at the distribution of gross earnings in April 1975 and compare it with one year earlier. I then examine basic wage rates, looking first at progress towards equal pay for women and then other settlements involving large numbers of low-paid workers. For the low paid the £30 a week government/Trades Union Congress minimum wage target was particularly relevant, and I try to assess whether the fixing of such targets helps or harms low earners. The final parts concentrate on more general issues. In the fourth section I examine how far settlements during the 1974-75 wage round kept within the government's cost of living pay limit guidelines. In the last one I turn to the current £6 a week pay limit and try to see how it looks like working out in the 1975-76 wages round and how pay policy might develop when this present phase expires in July 1976.

Earnings: April 1974 – April 1975

Before looking at the evidence of the official 1975 earnings survey I need to say something about the way in which this information is collected.

Clearly both employers and employees possess the information on earnings that is wanted. An ideal survey, therefore, might be expected to obtain information from both so as to cross check the accuracy of that provided by each. In practice, however, only employers are asked and there have been no details released of any attempts to find out the accuracy of the figures. Some employers, for example, do not provide any information. The response rate, 75% in 1975, has been declining in recent years and we do not know whether those paying particularly low wages predominate amongst those who do not respond. And of those who do provide data, some paying below statutory minimum scales may be inclined to overstate their employees' earnings and so inequalities will appear less.

On the other hand some of the earnings figures in the survey might be underestimated. First, the survey does not take account of the backdating of settlements. The recent substantial increase in the extent to which this has been practised means that possible errors on this score are becoming increasingly important, although the lowest paid, particularly in the private sector, are least likely to gain from sophisticated backdating agreements. Secondly, the annual earnings survey provides information on earnings received by an individual only from his main employer. The General Household Survey found that more than one worker in ten, and the low paid as much as

the rest, was 'moonlighting' i.e. had more than one paid job
(Office of Population Censuses and Surveys 1974). It is the
actual data, however, that I have to rely on here.

Table 2.1 sets out some of the main evidence. From the top
five rows it can be seen that at all levels of the distribution, from
the lowest to the highest, men's gross earnings increased by
some 28% between April 1974 and April 1975. What this
means is that the spread of earnings in percentage terms was
very much the same in both years. The absolute gap appeared
wider in 1975. Between £37.50 at the lowest decile (this is the
level below which are the poorest 10%) and £88.20 at the
highest was £50.70 and this was more than the £39.50 difference between these two same points in 1974. £50.70 in 1975
was, however, after taking account of inflation, worth not much
more than £39.50 was in 1974. So in absolute terms too there
was little change.

Table 2.1 also shows what happened to the gross earnings of
women. Whereas adult men, as we have seen, on average got
increases in gross weekly earnings of about 28% in 1974-75,
women did much better. They got, on average, rises of about
38%. It is true that every year I have reported that the gap
between women's and men's earnings has got narrower, at least
in percentage terms, but in 1974-75 this process was more
marked than before. That low-paid women considerably
improved their earnings relative to men can also be clearly seen
from the two columns in Table 2.1 showing the numbers of men
and women earning less than £40 a week in 1975 (the minimum
wage target proposed, though not agreed to, at the 1975 Trades
Union Congress) and the numbers earning less than £30 a week
in 1974 and £25 in 1973 (minimum wage targets accepted by
the Trades Union Congress in the respective years). On this
definition the number of low-paid men increased from 1.2
million in 1974 to 1.5 million in 1975 (a point taken up later),
but the number of low-paid women, by the same definition,
decreased from 3.5 million in 1974 to 3.2 million 1975.

Low-paid women, though their position improved compared
with men, could not keep up with their higher paid sisters. It
was the richest 10% of women who got most – a 43% increase
in 1974-75. It is because of this that, whereas men's earnings at
the level of the lowest decile slightly improved as a percentage
of median men's earnings, from 66.8% in 1974 to 67.0% in

Table 2.1   Dispersion of gross earnings of full-time adults in Great Britain

Weekly Earnings
ALL MEN (i.e. manual and non-manual)

	April 1975 £.p per week	April 1974 £.p per week	Increase 1974-75 %
10% (1.0 million) earning less than	37.50	29.30	28.0
25% (2.6 million) earning less than	45.30	35.40	28.0
50% (5.2 million) earning less than	55.90	43.80	27.6
25% (2.6 million) earning more than	70.10	54.60	28.4
10% (1.0 million) earning more than	88.20	68.80	28.2

ALL WOMEN

10% (0.5 million) earning less than	23.00	16.80	36.9
25% (1.2 million) earning less than	27.80	20.00	39.0
50% (2.4 million) earning less than	34.10	24.70	38.1
25% (1.2 million) earning more than	42.70	31.30	36.4
10% (0.5 million) earning more than	56.20	39.40	42.7

Numbers earning less than £40 a week in April 1975, £30 a week in April 1974 and £25 a week in April 1973

	ALL MEN (Millions)	ALL WOMEN (Millions)
1975	1.5	3.2
1974	1.2	3.5
1973	1.1	3.4

Weekly earnings at the level of the bottom tenth as percentage of the median

	ALL MEN	ALL WOMEN
1975	67.0	67.4
1974	66.8	67.7
1973	65.6	67.4

Hourly Earnings
For low-paid, average and high-paid manual and non-manual men and women in April 1975

	Manual Men £.p	Non-Manual Men £.p	Manual Women £.p	Non-Manual Women £.p
Lowest decile	0.86	0.99	0.56	0.64
Median	1.18	1.58	0.80	0.95
Highest decile	1.64	2.81	1.08	1.73

1975,women's earnings at the lowest dectile as a percentage of women's median earnings declined from 67.7% in 1974 to 67.4% in 1975.

So far I have concentrated on weekly earnings. The bottom three rows of Table 2.1 show the hourly pay of manual and non-manual full-time men and women. From this it can be seen that the lowest decile of manual men at 86p an hour earned just under one-third per hour of the highest decile of non-manual men who got £2.81 per hour; and this same 3:1 ratio roughly applied for women too – £1.73 at the highest decile of non-manual women and 56p at the lowest decile of manual women. Despite the wide differences in pay between men and women, the distribution of pay within each sex was roughly the same.

The bottom three rows in Table 2.1 also show differences between manual and non-manual earnings. From this it can be seen that, at the level of the lowest decile, non-manual men and women were only slightly better paid than manual workers. Only as one moves up towards higher paid workers does the manual/non-manual distinction become much more important. At the level of the highest decile non-manual workers earned 70% more per hour than manual ones. As my main concern here is low-paid men and women it will be sufficient to refer to them in aggregate, remembering that low pay applies almost as much to non-manual workers like clerks as to manual ones in agriculture, shops, hairdressers, laundries and the clothing trades.

Low pay I define, as in previous years, as earning less than two-thirds of average (median) earnings for all adult men working full time. This definition commands considerable support from public opinion (Behrend 1972) and has been adopted by the Low Pay Unit (Low Pay Unit 1975d). It meant in 1975 (to the nearest 50p) earning less than £37.50. It was roughly the bottom 10% of men earners and 60% of women who were low paid on this definition. £37.50 is also what the TUC minimum wage target fixed at £30 in 1974 would have been worth in 1975 after taking account of the 25% rise in prices.

Table 2.1 shows that one million men earned less than £37.50 in April 1975 compared to 1.2 million men earning less than £30 in April 1974. This seems to show that there were fewer low paid than a year earlier. The data refer, however, only to full-time workers so, to the extent that in 1975 low-paid workers

were more likely than better off ones to have been on short time
or unemployed, they would have dropped out of the picture
altogether. Things would then appear brighter for the low paid
than they really were. The combined effect of less full-time
workers and the lower response rate in 1975 is that there were in
the 1975 survey only 10.3 million full-time adult men and 4.7
million adult women compared to 10.7 and 5.0 respectively in
1974. The annual earnings survey therefore does not allow us to
say for certain whether the problem of low pay was getting
worse or better.

Wage rates
The distribution of earnings as it was in April 1975, so far
discussed, was in large part due to the wage settlements made
during the 1974-75 wage round. During that period the Trades
Union Congress (TUC) promised that they would do all they
could to ensure that pay increases did no more than compensate for rises in the cost of living (Trades Union Congress
1974). Extra increases in wage rates were allowed, however, for
moving towards equal pay and for the low paid. Before examining how well this voluntary incomes policy worked overall I
need to discuss them. Wage rates for women are certainly
important. As already indicated, women predominate amongst
the low paid. About a quarter of all full-time men earned less
than £45 a week in April 1975, compared with three-quarters of
full-time women.

From 29 December 1975 it was illegal not to give equal pay to
men and women employed on work of the same or similar
nature. The Equal Pay Act which brought this about passed
into law in 1970, but the gap between men and women's rates at
that time was very wide indeed and it was thought best to have
a five-year transition period to facilitate 'orderly progress'. As it
turned out the progress was very disorderly. In agriculture, for
example, women's rates were 80% of men's in 1972 and still at
that level in March 1975; only in the last six months of the five
years were steps taken to close this gap, and even then the
advance was limited for part-time women workers, because a
new special lower hourly rate was introduced for them. It is still
too early, at the time of writing, to look at how the Act is
operating now it is fully in force, but I can look at what
happened in the 1974-75 wage round.

The best source of information on progress on wage rates is the Department of Employment's (DE) register of national agreements and wages orders, maintained specifically for the purpose of officially monitoring the implementation of the Equal Pay Act. The official view of the 1974-75 period is that 'the DE Register shows that . . . considerable progress has been made'. More precisely, whereas only one in twenty of the agreements and orders had women's rates over 90% of the men's rate for the same job in March 1970, the proportion was six out of ten by March 1974 and nine out of every ten by March 1975. At the level of individual companies the Department's surveys found 'a quickening trend towards the removal of discrimination' (Department of Employment 1975b). Of course some employers are obstinately refusing to give equal pay, and at the plant level the Department singles out for specific criticisms parts of the food, drink and tobacco industry and parts of the distributive trades. It is also true that where men's rates are very low as in laundries, hairdressing and the clothing trades, for example, then the gains for women are limited. Nevertheless there do seem to have been considerable gains for many low-paid women at work – at least those who have kept their jobs.

Minimum wages
For the low paid a main clause of the social contract guidelines was, and remains, the minimum wage target of £30 for a 40-hour week. This target, agreed in September 1974, was intended to be of real benefit to the low paid. At that time it represented 62% of average earnings and a floor at that level would certainly have been a big achievement. Unfortunately, it has not since then been revised upwards to take account of inflation or the general rise in earnings. By September 1975, £30 a week represented only 49% of average earnings and by August 1976, when the next phase of the pay policy is due to start, it will be down to 39%; to that extent it is inadequate as a minimum wage target.

Independent of the level, however, the very concept of a minimum wage target officially recognised by the government is new. What effect, if any, has this had? It is of course impossible to say for certain, because we do not know what would have happened if it had not existed. Nevertheless, there is evidence that it has had some effect. The organisation Industrial Relations in their twice monthly *Review and Report* present a league table of the basic weekly wage rates for the lowest grade of male manual worker in over 100 of the larger national negotiating groups (those with over 10,000 employees). In July 1975 this table showed that 12 groups which settled between September 1974 and June 1975, including local authorities, national health service ancillaries, wholesale grocery and food manufacturing, all agreed on minimum rates exactly equal to the government/TUC minimum wage target of £30 a week. A year earlier these same 12 groups had different basic wage rates, from Soap, Candle and Edible Fat at £20.24 to Ready Mixed Concrete at £25.54. Moreover, a year earlier in July 1974 it was also true that there was no one figure in the entire league table on which more than four different groups agreed.

The fact that these 12 previously scattered groups all converged on £30 a week at the end of the 1974-75 winter wage round suggests that the minimum wage rate target did affect negotiators' behaviour and the resulting settlements. It could be, however, that this was for the worse rather than the better. Without it they might have got more. But for many of the low paid this seems doubtful in the light of a Low Pay Unit survey in this period which showed that the majority of settlements for low-paid workers (62 out of 82) were above the average percentage for all workers (Low Pay Unit 1975b).

So the low paid have overall been doing somewhat better recently. Not all of them, however, shared in this progress to the same degree and some not at all. The Low Pay Unit survey identified a public/private split, as can be seen from the following evidence on the basis of an analysis of 82 major agreements involving low-paid workers, defined as those with less than £30 a week in 1974 (Low Pay Unit 1975b).

Low pay settlements under the social contract

	Public Sector	Private Sector	Wages Council	Total
Above average	26	18	18	62
Below average	3	5	12	20

Note: Average means average percentage increase for all workers including those not low-paid.

This shows that progress for the low paid was most marked

Table 2.2 Wage increases for some low-paid groups in 1974, 1975 and, where already decided, 1976

Group of workers and numbers covered	Weekly wage rate before 1973-74 winter wage round £.p	Increase from 1973-74 winter wage round £.p	Weekly wage rate before 1974-75 winter wage round £.p	Increase from 1974-75 winter wage round £.p	Weekly wage rate before 1975-76 winter wage round £.p	Increase from 1975-76 winter wage round £.p	Weekly wage rate in summer of 1976 £.p
Public Sector							
Nurses 340,000	15.69	5.94	21.63	8.37	30.00	?	?
Local Authority Manuals 1,000,000	19.85	2.32	22.17	7.83	30.00	6.00	36.00
NHS Ancillaries 220,000	19.88	2.40	22.28	7.72	30.00	6.00	36.00
Ambulancemen 16,000	21.20	2.27	23.47	8.53	32.00	6.00	38.00
Private							
Tailoring 94,000	16.32	1.80	18.12	4.80	22.92	3.60	26.52
Dressmaking 93,000	16.30	1.80	18.10	4.80	22.90	?	?
Laundry 78,000	14.20	1.66	15.86	6.35	22.00	5.90	27.90
Hairdressing 140,000	13.30	1.80	14.10	5.25	19.35	?	?

in the public sector, less so in the non-wages councils part of the private sector and even less in the wages council sector which is also predominantly private.

Because I cannot in the space available consider in detail all the settlements involving low-paid workers, what I have done is to pick out eight to illustrate the general pattern and in particular this public/private split. Table 2.2 shows the size of the settlements and the level of the new weekly wage rates agreed for 1974, 1975 and where possible 1976. From this it can be seen that, whereas some nurses have already had a 90% increase in pay since 1974, many workers in the clothing trades got less than £2 a week more in the 1973-74 wages round, less than £5 a week more in that of 1974-75, and less than £4 a week more in the current one, and as a result their minimum rates for the late summer of 1975 were still well below the £30 minimum wage target fixed in 1974. Obviously, this is not to decry the progress made for the low paid in the public sector. Nurses in particular were long overdue in getting these improvements. It is just unfortunate that many other deserving groups, particularly in the private sector, have not been so lucky.

Even where above average increases were granted by Wages Councils, as for example in industrial and staff canteens where the minimum rates were raised by almost 50% in 1975, the new levels are still low: £19.80. The Low Pay Unit point out in their *Bulletin* in July 1975 that 'no wages council settlement reached during the first six months of 1975 has agreed on a minimum rate which is equal to the TUC target of £30 a week, a target which was set in Autumn 1974'. The breakdown of all wages councils awards for that period shows that the minimum male adult rate was still below £20 in nine cases, £20 to £25 in eighteen, £25 to £30 in three, and none above £30. There is, moreover, now much evidence to show that these minimum rates set by the councils determine what large numbers of low-paid workers actually get (Low Pay Unit 1975c; Trinder 1974).

Cost of living pay increases
The social contract was supposed to limit pay rises to price rises. Did it succeed? Most commentators think it did not. *The Economist* (1975), citing the fact that the overall index of hourly wage rates was rising much faster than prices, concluded that

'any small boy in the crowd can see that the social contract, like the Emperor, is naked'. This view was reinforced by the organisation Industrial Relations which looked at 52 individual settlements agreed during the period and reported that 'the main conclusion' of their survey was that 'most workers have been receiving increases far in excess of price rises', although they were not precise on what 'far in excess' meant (Industrial Relations 1975). For the government, Mr Healey was also broadly of the same opinion and he did put a figure on the 'gap'. In his Budget speech (15 April 1975) he acknowledged that 'many in the trade union movement have worked hard to apply the guidelines' but he added that this had not been enough to ensure success. The result was that 'the general rate of pay increases has been well above the increase in the cost of living – pay has been running 8% to 9% ahead of prices. I do not believe that anyone would claim that the TUC guidelines were intended to permit this result . . . rates of increase which ought to have been exceptional have been applied to others who have no justification.'

No one would claim that the contract was watertight, but statements like those just quoted exaggerated its failure. The way in which the overall excesses were measured made the policy look leakier than it was. *The Economist* (1975) compared a 33% rise in hourly wage rates between April 1974 and April 1975 with the 21% rise in prices March 1974 to March 1975. If they had waited for the full data to become available, and had then compared the earnings and prices from July 1974 to July 1975, the increases would have been 27% and 26% respectively. What is more, as already explained, movement towards equal pay and rises up to a basic minimum of £30 for a 40-hour week were explicitly allowed by the guidelines on top of cost of living rises. Many employers previously slipping behind in implementing equal pay made up the lost ground in the winter of 1974-75 (Department of Employment 1975b). The government actuary in October 1975 estimated that the movement towards equal pay alone will add almost 2% to the earnings total in the £6 pay limit wages round (*Hansard* 23 October 1975). Similar estimates were not made in earlier years but the £gures may have applied in 1974-75 too.

Finally, the survey by the Low Pay Unit showed that just over three-quarters of all settlements involving workers on less than the basic £30 a week minimum legitimately took advantage of the clause permitting them to increase pay for the lower paid by more than the increase in the cost of living (Low Pay Unit 1975b). The total amount which all these different types of legitimate extras would have been expected to add to the earnings total is not known, but it is unlikely that Mr Healey's 8% to 9% gap between earnings and prices would remain after taking them into account.

On the more specific subject of which settlements broke the guidelines, Michael Foot stated that 25% of the agreements were outside them, but he would not go further and say which settlements or by how much. Incomes Data Services provide the most comprehensive detailed information about wage settlements during each year. For the winter wage round of 1974-75 they looked at 106 settlements covering well over 11 million workers. On the basis of this evidence they concluded that on average the level of public sector pay awards was running 6% above that of private sector agreements and that the gap was widening (Incomes Data Services 1975). Tim Congdon in *The Times* (11 July 1975) challenged this view, however, pointing to a number of 'special cases' representing a once-and-for-all movement rather than a trend, and arguing that what might be true for wage rates, which was what Incomes Data Services were looking at, was not so in terms of earnings. So perhaps we are no nearer to finding out which settlements were outside the guidelines. Certainly many people felt that the much publicised railwaymen's and miners' were.

But the guidelines were vague. Tom Jackson argued that threshold payments were for the previous year's price rises and that it was 'new money' that counted. On this basis he stated in *The Listener* (1975) that at the lowest rates the £2.60 'new money' for the railwaymen was low compared to earlier settlements which gave £3.10 to postmen, £3.30 to local authority manual workers, £4 to water and also gas workers, £4.50 to company busmen and £5.30 to British Airways workers. Thus a major indictment of the voluntary policy then in force was that because it was so unclear it was open to many different interpretations. Fortunately the TUC has itself subsequently learned from past mistakes and now publicly recognises that this imprecision caused problems which 'helped to weaken the previous policy' and adds that a major virtue of the 'universal application of the figures of £6 per week' is that 'it is clear and simple' (Trades Union Congress 1975).

The £6 pay limit and beyond

In June 1975, the government issued an ultimatum to the TUC that unless they came up with pay guidelines that would stick then the government would act unilaterally. The TUC, and Jack Jones in particular, responded by putting forward proposals for flat-rate increases for one year with nothing extra for those already on relatively high incomes. In July the government released its White Paper, *The Attack on Inflation*, which fixed the details: 'relatively high' meant £8,500 a year and the level of rises for those on less than this was to be £6 a week with proportionate increases for part-time and junior workers. The government also made it clear that 'the policy will operate from the beginning of the next pay round', roughly from 1 August 1975 to 31 July 1976, and that during this period the 12-month interval between major pay increases, which should have been a major feature of the first phase of the social contract, will continue to apply.

The £6 is an individual limit. Unlike under the previous incomes policies of Mr Heath, a firm will be breaching the guidelines if it pays any employees over the £6 (apart from incremental pay rises and women moving to equal pay) even if it keeps its overall wage bill for those earning less than £8,500 to an average of £6 per week. Moreover the £6 is an earnings supplement, as were the threshold payments of Mr Heath's policy. It is not an addition to the basic rates and cannot therefore be used for calculating overtime rates or holiday pay. Any improvements in holidays or other non-wage benefits has to be offset against the pay figures, the only exemption being for increases in employers' contributions to occupational pension schemes. There is this time no special provision for the low paid because the flat-rate formula is itself of potentially great benefit to them. A £6 increase to a worker on £24 a week represents a 25% rise, but for one on £7,500 a year only a 4% one. The ratio of 6:1 is reduced to 5:1 simply by both workers getting the £6. Moreover, although it is true that in absolute terms the differences in pay remain the same – the gap between £24 and £50 in 1975 and between £30 and £56 in 1976 is still £26 – that £26 is, because of inflation, worth much less in 1976 than it was in

1975. The government's view of course is that the £6 is a maximum within which negotiations can take place; the White Paper emphasises that 'some employers may not be able to pay it'.

There are, however, five main types of exception to these general rules. First, as stated earlier, those already earning more than £8,500 a year cannot have any more pay at all unless this stems from promotion or re-grading exercises agreed before 11 July 1975. Second, increases of more than £6 for women are permitted where these derive from movements towards equal pay which by law had to be achieved by 29 December 1975. Third, the 2½ million workers in the public sector and two million in the private already covered by well established incremental or wage-for-age pay scales can have rises which take their total increase over the year to over the £6 provided 'this does not raise the overall wage bill by more than £6 per head'. Fourth, ongoing productivity schemes such as that of the miners can go ahead unaltered and provide increases above the £6 pay limit, as can incomes resulting from extra overtime. Finally, index-linked settlements such as that already agreed for post office workers will be allowed whatever the amounts involved, but in this case payments over and above £6 a week will have to be set against the next annual settlement. These exceptions to the general rules, especially allowing annual increments on top of the £6, may well dilute the benefit for the lowest paid, particularly those in manual jobs. Moreover, this trend could be aggravated still further, as the Trade Union Research Unit at Ruskin College, Oxford, have pointed out in one of a series of reports on the effects of recent pay policies. Even some of the low-paid who do get the full £6 will not benefit because, with the recession there is likely to be less overtime, more short time and more unemployment and the unskilled are the most vulnerable (Trade Union Research Unit 1975). So it is only a qualified welcome that I can give the new £6 pay policy, and the package of which it forms part needs to be assessed as a whole.

At the time of writing no breaches of the £6 limit were apparent and most workers, including many low-paid groups particularly in the public sector, appeared to be settling for the full amount. A million local authority manual workers settled for a £6 a week pay increase for all as from November 1975. The

lowest grades, including car park attendants, lavatory attendants and some cleaners, were previously on the minimum
wage target level of £30 a week. Some wages boards and wages
councils too were raising statutory minimum rates by the full £6
earnings supplement, although on closer inspection it seemed
that some of their workers were still missing out. One example
is the wages council covering 270,000 workers in non-
residential licensed restaurants, clubs and pubs, a group of very
low-paid workers (Trinder 1974). Among these, adult workers
(defined as those aged 20 years or over) get the full £6 but those
aged 18-20 years only £5.40. Many workers in this industry are
in the latter age group. Since the government's White Paper
The Attack on Inflation is quite clear that 'adults are those aged 18
years or over', these workers are, on the TUC interpretation of
the guidelines, 'being deprived of their full entitlement'.

In fact many of the wages boards and councils have their own
definitions for who should get the full amount. In agriculture,
for example, adults are again those aged 20 years or over and in
hairdressing the age is 22 years. Learners and apprentices are
sometimes excluded even if older than this, and, even for those
who qualified on all these counts, allowable deductions for
board and lodging were often substantially raised at the same
time, for example by 50p to £1.50 for a tied cottage in agriculture, so that not everyone did in fact get the full £6 a week pay
increase.

In addition, as Michael Foot said, 5% of the workers covered
by all settlements got amounts 'significantly less' than £6 (*Hansard* 28 October 1975) and these could have particularly
included the low paid. Although it is not clear what 'significantly less' means, and despite TUC promises to monitor
settlements, there is little information about who these workers
are except that they are all in the private sector (*Hansard* 2
December 1975). They may include supermarket staff in the
retail grocery trade, who received from November 1975 a supplement of £5.20 on existing rates, bringing the lowest grades
up to a minimum of £30 a week, a year after many other
workers. They would certainly include the garment and tailor-
ing workers, another very low-paid group (Trinder 1975), who
accepted increases of only £3.60 a week. It looks likely that once
again those who need it most, particularly in the private sector,
are the ones who get least. But with many settlements still to

come it is too early to be certain.

The government made it clear in *The Attack on Inflation* that they intend to maintain an incomes policy 'over a number of years'. The form that this should take has already been subject to considerable speculation, but the official view re-echoed by Mr Wilson on 14 October 1975, the day after parliament recommenced after the summer recess, was that it was still too early to say. He merely confirmed that 'during the year [August 1975-July 1976] – well before the end of that year, we will have to consider the situation for the next and succeeding years'. It is to be hoped, however, that he will not wait too long, that a full public debate will precede any decision and that a rush like that which preceded the launching of the £6 pay limit policy in July 1975 will be avoided. Full discussion is especially important because of the widely differing opinions on what should be done. The TUC recognises that £6 a week rises 'is a temporary policy put forward for the coming year to arrest the inflationary process, prevent massive unemployment and enable the Labour Government to carry out its industrial programme. It is certainly not envisaged as a permanent policy for continually eroding differentials either between or within negotiating groups' (Trades Union Congress 1975). They may not, however go all the way with Mr Healey or the National Institute that it will be essential to restore lost differentials 'to some degree' (National Institute of Economic and Social Research 1975).

Conclusions

The points I would stress are, first, that during the social contract period some low-paid workers, especially those in the public sector, have seen considerable advances in their relative gross pay. There has been much debate recently about the rate of growth of the public sector wage bill. This chapter shows that it was not just the already high-paid civil servant who got increases. At the same time, however, many other low-paid workers have become worse off. Particularly for example in the clothing trades, retail distribution, hairdressing and other parts of the private sector, the low paid continue to do very badly. This public/private split may be the unintentional outcome of an economic recession which has left many employers on the land and in textiles unable to pay more, but it need not and must not continue. Public opinion polls in 1973 showed that twice as many people cited agricultural workers as most deserving of substantial pay rises than they did nurses (Behrend 1974). Yet it was the nurses who got an independent Halsbury inquiry into their pay and conditions and as a result massive pay rises. Agricultural workers by contrast are still being refused such an independent inquiry, though they are now in relative terms worse off than they were ten years ago and there is much poverty amongst their familes (Trinder and Winyard 1975; Brown and Winyard 1975). During the next phase of the pay policy it is essential that a more overall view is taken of low pay and that workers in the private sector are brought into the reckoning as much as those in the public.

The need for a comprehensive focus brings me to my second point. An overall view is needed not just at a point in time, but over time too. I mentioned last year the Low Pay Unit's proposal for a strategy for abolishing low pay over, say, a five-year period. There are far too many low-paid workers and many of them are so far below two-thirds of average earnings that no solution on the cheap is possible, while no solution that is expensive will be acceptable for completion in 1976 alone. For the low paid really to narrow the gap between them and the average, much more than a once-and-for-all declaration is required. The government realised this on equal pay for men and women and phased this in over the 1970-75 period. Let it be realised for low pay in the same way in 1976 to 1980.

My final point is that it is not just gross pay that counts. The government needs to look at the way in which tax policy takes away with one hand what its pay policy gives with the other. In March 1975 a married man at work with two children began to pay tax when his income reached £25 a week, £5 below the government/TUC minimum wage target. When his income reached £27 this family was in the absurd position of paying 70p to the Inland Revenue in tax, while claiming 50p family income supplement from the Department of Health and Social Security (Pond 1975). In the end it is changing living standards that count and, as I show in the next chapter, one needs to take account of much else besides gross income.

References

A.B. Atkinson (1975) *The Economics of Inequality*, Oxford University Press

H. Behrend (1972) 'Public acceptability and a workable incomes policy' in F. Blackaby (ed.) *An Incomes Policy for Britain*, Heinemann

H. Behrend (1974) *Attitudes to Price Increases and Pay Claims*, National Economic Development Office Monograph 4, NEDO November 1974

M. Brown and S. Winyard (1975) *Low Pay on the Farm*, Low Pay Pamphlet 3, Low Pay Unit

Department of Employment (1975a), *New Earnings Survey 1975*, HMSO

Department of Employment (1975b), 'Further progress towards equal pay', *Department of Employment Gazette* September 1975, HMSO

Department of Health and Social Security (1975), *Two-Parent Families Receiving Family Income Supplement*, Statistical and Research Report no. 9, HMSO

The Economist (1975) 'The next social contract', 26 April 1975

Incomes Data Services (1975) 'Review of settlements' *Report No. 212* July 1975, Incomes Data Services

Industrial Relations (1975) 'The social contract and the winter wages round' *Review and Report* no. 100, Industrial Relations

T. Jackson (1975) 'Reporting pay awards', *Listener* 14 August 1975

Low Pay Unit (1975a) *Employment Protection Bill*, Briefing Notes nos. 1-7, Low Pay Unit

Low Pay Unit (1975b) 'The low pay contract', *Low Pay Bulletin* no. 2, Low Pay Unit

Low Pay Unit (1975c) 'Low pay awards' *Low Pay Bulletin* no. 4 Low Pay Unit

Low Pay Unit (1975d) 'Low pay diary' *Low Pay Bulletin* no. 6 Low Pay Unit

National Institute of Economic and Social Research (1975), *Quarterly Review* November 1975, National Institute of Economic and Social Research

Office of Population Censuses and Surveys (1974) *General Household Survey*, HMSO

C. Pond (1975) *Taxing the Social Contract*, Low Pay Unit Paper no. 2, Low Pay Unit

The Attack on Inflation (1975) Cmnd 6151, HMSO

Trades Union Congress (1974) *Collective Bargaining and the Social Contract*, Trades Union Congress

Trades Union Congress (1975) *The Development of the Social Contract*, Trades Union Congress

Trades Union Research Unit (1975) *10% or £6: Some Pay Bill Arithmetic*, Trades Union Research Unit, Ruskin College, Oxford, July 1975

C. Trinder (1974) 'Low pay at the bar', *Poverty* no. 25, Summer 1974, Child Poverty Action Group

C. Trinder (1975) *A Stitch in Time: Proposals for the Reform of the Clothing Wages Councils*, Low Pay Unit Paper no. 5, Low Pay Unit

C. Trinder and S. Winyard (1975) *A New Deal for Farmworkers*, Low Pay Unit Paper no. 6, Low Pay Unit

*For a proper assessment of people's changing circum-
stances, one needs to take account of the effect on gross
wages of taxes, national insurance contributions,
prices, subsidies and allowances. When these are
brought into the reckoning, how did poorer earners fare?*

3   Inflation and the working poor
CHRIS TRINDER

Inflation is currently the overriding issue. Its causes and possible cures are much discussed. But the immediate concern must
be with the effects, especially on the poor, of inflation and of the
policies to combat it. Have the low-paid worker and his family
been hit harder than others by the rise in prices in 1975 or has
the inflation simply drawn attention to the low level from which
they began? With notable exceptions (Townsend 1975; Liesner
and King 1975) questions such as these have been relatively
neglected.

My analysis in this chapter concentrates on the position of
the lowest-paid workers, though here, as in the previous chapter, they clearly must be seen in relation to the rest of the
population. In the first section I look at the effects of inflation
on changing tax burdens; in the second I turn to prices directly
and look at the cost of living of the poor; in the third I take
account of means-tested benefits and examine the so-called
'poverty trap'; in the fourth I bring all these parts together and
try to sum up what has happened to the living standards of the
working poor in the year of inflation, 1975.

Changing tax burdens
Taxes are of two types – direct and indirect. The latter directly
influence prices and are discussed in the next section. The
former, made up mainly of income tax and national insurance
contributions, play a large part in determining take-home pay.
Changes in direct taxes are usually made in the spring Budget

and it is with Mr Healey's in April 1975 that I begin. The overriding theme both in the Budget speech and throughout the preceding months was that because 'wages and salaries have risen overall substantially above what was envisaged by the (TUC) guidelines, I therefore have no alternative but to raise the income tax' (*Hansard* 15 April 1975).

What Mr Healey did was to raise the basic rate by 2% from 33% in 1974-75 to 35% in 1975-76, which itself reduced demand by £770 million in a full year; he also increased by 2% all the higher rates except the top one, which remained unaltered at 83% for earned income and 98% for investment income. He refrained from increasing tax allowances, so that, in a period of inflation and with the present tax structure, the tax burdens are automatically rising over time. The child tax allowances were left exactly as in 1974-75, although their money value did rise slightly as a result of the tax rate going up from 33% to 35%. The single person's or wife's earnings allowance was increased by £50, equivalent to 8%, the married man's by £90, equal to 10%, but this was much less than the rate of inflation. The result was that in real terms all allowances were worth substantially less in 1975-76 than they had been previously. The overall effect was severe tax increases for the worker with average earnings. If he was a married man with two children, income tax claimed 13.5% of his income in 1974-75, but 17.7% in 1975-76.

The Chancellor justified his actions by saying that the effect 'of excessive wage settlements is to increase private consumption, with damaging effects on the balance of resources in the economy, which the government must seek to remove by increasing taxation', and he made it clear that these changes in tax burdens were to 'be regarded as an anti-inflation surcharge'. But who bore the brunt?

Mr Healey was not being entirely honest when he described the changes in tax rates and allowances for the lowest paid as 'reducing their tax burdens' and 'taking 400,000 people out of tax' altogether. Sam Brittan, in the *Financial Times* (16 April 1975), produced a table of income tax liabilities for 1974-75 and 1975-76, adjusted for inflation. As a result of the Budget the effective tax rate for a family with two children on £30 a week almost doubled in percentage terms, rising from 4.6% of total income to 8.1%. For a family with the same number of children on £5,000 per annum, tax as a percentage of total income rose only from 24.5% to 27.0%. As one moved from lower to higher incomes it was quite clear that the additional tax burdens fell disproportionately on the lowest paid.

Mr Healey was able to maintain that some tax burdens were being reduced only because he totted up the amount of taxes due (at an annual rate) on the day before and day after the Budget (a trap which most newspapers, apart from *The Financial Times*, still fall into each year on the morning after the Budget). This failed to take account of the fact that the tax changes run for a full year during which time earnings and prices also change.

The Chancellor therefore did levy additional tax burdens onto the low-paid worker and his family. But might he have done it because he felt that the tax system was already taking too much from well-off people compared with those on lower incomes? Clearly not, for in November 1974 he had said that 'The main instrument for achieving the necessary redistribution of wealth and income is our system of personal taxation . . . the time for dealing with this will be in the Spring [1975] Budget'. New light was shed on this question with the publication of the first report of the Royal Commission on the Distribution of Income and Wealth (1975). The Royal Commission had compiled special evidence on the distributional effect of income tax in the 1970s; their report showed the distribution of income before and after tax in 1972-73. The relevant figures are reproduced in Table 3.1, which divides tax payers into the wealthiest 10%, poorest 20% etc; the first column shows the way the total of gross income was shared out amongst these groups, and the second their respective shares of what was left after each had met their tax liabilities.

Table 3.1   Distribution of income before and after tax 1972-73

% of income units	*% of total income*	
	Before income tax	*After income tax*
Top 10%	27%	24%
Next 30%	40%	40%
Next 40%	27%	29%
Bottom 20%	6%	7%

The table shows for instance that the poorest 20% of incomes accounted for 6% of all incomes before tax was deducted and 7% – very much the same – after. The richest 10% of incomes accounted for 27% of all pre-tax income and 24% – not much less – of post-tax income. The Royal Commission commented that they were perturbed 'that the proportion of total personal income received by the 20% group of lowest income recipients had changed little since the end of the 1950s'. No wonder that in outlining their future programme of work they said that this matter deserved further study.

National insurance contributions are in many ways simply another form of direct taxation, so the combined effect needs to be taken into account. There were important changes in insurance contributions in 1975. The Social Security Act 1975 requires the Secretary of State for Social Services to review every year from now on the general level of earnings in Britain and to consider what changes in national insurance contributions need to be made in the light of this and other relevant factors.

At present earnings-related contributions are levied at a rate of 5½% from employees and 8½% from employers on earnings of more than £13 a week, up to a level of £69 (above which no additional contribution is levied). In October 1975 Barbara Castle announced that from April 1976 the upper limit of earnings on which contributions are paid would be £95, an increase of about 30%. She also said that the rates of contribution from employees would be raised to 5¾% and from employers to 8¾% for all earnings above £13 a week. Barbara Castle defined the overall effect of these changes as adding 15p a week to the total contributions levied on the worker earning £60 a week and proportionately less for those with lower earnings. She was however adopting the same totting up procedure, ignoring inflation, that I mentioned earlier. In fact after allowing for the man on £30 a week to be earning £36 a week in 1976, ie an increase in his pay of £6 a week, he would as a result of changes pay 42p more in national insurance contributions. This increase, as a proportion of his total income, is much greater than the 50p extra which the man on £60 in 1975 and £66 in 1976 would pay.

On the subject of the ceiling level above which earnings-related national insurance contributions are not levied, Mr

Healey cited the government defeat on the earnings rule for pensioners. The defeat meant that retired people could in 1975 earn up to £20 a week without their pension being reduced, a figure which rises to £35 in 1976 and £50 in 1977. Mr Healey argued that the extra cost of this change, £60 million in 1975-76 and £110 million in 1976-77, would have to be met by increasing the ceiling by £8 a week more than otherwise would have been the case (presumably it would have gone up to £87 rather than £95). He said that 'in this way the cost will be met without imposing extra burdens on the less well-off contributors'. The Child Poverty Action Group (CPAG) and others, however, viewed these changes differently and in particular felt that there should not be an upper limit at all on earnings for which earnings-related contributions are levied. In November 1975 the government actuary revealed that abolishing this ceiling would yield £480 million extra revenue and that this could be used to raise substantially the level of pay (from April 1976, £13 a week) at which people start paying earnings-related contributions; doing this would genuinely allow the burdens on the less well off to be reduced.

The incidence of national insurance contributions also needs looking at more carefully than hitherto. Burdens have typically been assessed as though the nominal incidence (from April 1976, 5¾% from employees and 8¾% from employers) is all borne by the respective parties, and as though there is no scope for shifting it to other groups. In fact the employer's extra contributions might to some extent be borne by his employees if as a result he grants smaller pay rises, or some of the burden might be shifted onto the consumer in the form of higher prices. The Social Security Act 1975 lays down that in 1978 the rates will rise to an employer's contribution of 10% and an employee's of 6.5%. The amounts involved are far too large to be allocated in the rather casual fashion currently used; a fuller understanding of who actually pays is a prerequisite of any comprehensive study of overall changes in tax burdens.

Prices and the poor
1975 was the first full year of operation of the Department of Prices and Consumer Protection. It was also a year in which a new National Consumer Council was formed under the chairmanship of Michael Young, and in which the Department of

Employment spent more money than ever before explaining how the official retail price index is constructed, why it was going up so fast, and what the government was doing to try to bring the annual rate of increase down from 26% in July 1975 to 10% in the autumn of 1976 and to less than 10% by the end of the year (Department of Employment 1975a and 1975b).

Given this growing official interest in prices generally, it might have been expected that attention would be given to whether low income consumers were facing special problems. This was not done. In *Poverty Report 1974* Tony Atkinson and I argued that there was at that time a strong case for the publication of official price indices for different groups (in addition to the official pensioner's index), since the single retail price index might well mask divergent movements for different types of household. If the British government did this they would not be the first. In Germany there was already an official price index for low-paid workers and another for high-paid workers in addition to the average index. Pond's unofficial look at the subject in Britain suggested that the cost of living of the poor had in 1975 again started to rise faster than that of the rich (Pond 1975). The report of the Royal Commission on the Distribution of Income and Wealth included a section on the adequacy of existing price indices for measuring the cost of living of the poor and concluded that 'this is an area in which we hope to see more work done in the future' (Royal Commission on the Distribution of Income and Wealth 1975). But, apart from the retired persons' index, there were still at the end of 1975 no official cost of living indices for the poor.

So the government did not make any progress on this during the year. But what about action on prices? It was estimated that the cost of food subsidies in 1975-76 was £554 million. But this did not mean that the prices of basic foods remained stable. Milk went up from 5p to 6p to 7p and then from 2 November to 8½p a pint. The 2p a pint subsidy meant only that at the end of the year it would otherwise have been 10½p a pint. For some of the other subsidised foods the picture was similar. Bread, for example, at 17p for a large loaf in December 1975 was 3p more than in January despite a 2p subsidy; the average price of cheese was 48p a pound in December, despite a 12p a pound subsidy, partly due to the devaluation of the 'green pound' during the year; this compared with 40p a pound in January.

With butter now subsidised by 11p a pound and tea by 8p a pound any speedy phasing out of subsidies would mean more severe increases in prices. The government revealed in 1975 that if food subsidies were withdrawn immediately this would add 73p a week to the bills of the average family of two adults and two children (*Hansard* 25 November 1975).

It is not just food prices, but also housing costs and fuel prices that are particularly important to the poor. On housing Chris Holmes reports in Chapter 7, but I would add that rate increases in 1975 were in some areas the largest annual increases ever, and with the ending of the rent freeze in March 1975 housing costs rose on this count too. On fuel prices, domestic gas went up 34%, electricity 50% and coal 55½% in the 12 months ending 31 October 1975 (*Hansard* 11 November 1975). These increases were much more than the overall rate of price increase of 26% during this period, and were the direct result of the change in government policy which now instructs the nationalised industries to charge commercial prices and cover their own costs rather than rely on subsidies from the Exchequer.

At the time of the Budget much was made of Mr Healey replacing the 8% single rate of VAT which applied to luxuries and necessities alike with a new 25% rate which applied not just to petrol but also to 'electrical appliances, other than cookers, space heaters and water heaters; to radios, television sets, hi-fi and similar equipment; to boats, aircraft and caravans, to cameras and binoculars and to furs and jewellery' – in the Chancellor's words 'less necessary goods'. Despite this welcome measure, the overall rise in the price of durable goods as measured by the relevant component in the retail price index March to October 1975 was 14% compared to one of 19% for housing and 23% for fuel and light. The increase in the price of beer by 2p a pint and cigarettes by 7p for 20, also announced in the Budget, increased these prices even more, and, whatever the health arguments for deterring consumption of these, the poor still spend a larger share of their income on them than do the rich, so this burden too falls more heavily on the worst off.

The question of prices and the poor is a matter not just of how fast the prices are rising, but also concerns the level of prices in the first place. The old person who uses his telephone only occasionally but whose need for it is primarily in case of emergency, has to pay the same fixed charge as everyone else, except that as a proportion of total cost the charge is much higher. Much the same applies to users of small amounts of gas and electricity. There is also the question of the cost of living for those, for example, who cannot travel far and have to shop at their corner shop rather than go to the supermarket. It was the disproportionate price of 2½p for an individual fish finger which attracted the attention of the newspapers, but Age Concern has shown that for food overall pensioners often get much less value, £ for £ (Age Concern 1974).

The first National Consumer Congress held in Manchester in September 1975 devoted more than half of its agenda to the problems facing low income consumers and the extent to which the poor pay more was one of the major questions which it examined (National Consumer Council 1975). In 1976 Shirley Williams aims to tackle part of this problem by local price-watch surveys and many local authorities have now agreed to take part, but the problem is more than just knowing where the best buys are. It is to be hoped that new initiatives to help poorer consumers will come before long.

The poverty trap

So far I have discussed the taxes and prices. In many ways, however, it is the overlap between income tax and income maintenance which causes most problems in trying to abolish poverty. The extensive use of means-tested benefits and the lowering of the tax threshold has meant that in recent years many of the poor have been trapped in their poverty.

In last year's *Poverty Report*, for example, I calculated the total effect of various changes over the year October 1973 to October 1974 for a low-paid worker with four children who had had a 20% increase in gross pay. I took into account inflation, tax and national insurance contributions (and changes in thresholds during the year) and means-tested benefits such as family income supplement (FIS) and rent and rate rebates (including changes in income limits for eligibility that occurred during the year). I showed that during the year the family would have failed to maintain its standard of living even at the low level it was at in October 1973. In fact by Octobeer 1974 it would have declined by about 1%. Even if the father had increased his gross pay by 29% (9% more than the 20% assumed above), his real disposable resources would have increased by only some 1% because of the corresponding withdrawal of means-tested benefits and the extra tax due.

No one disputes the existence of the poverty trap in the past. In 1972, after the Conservative government introduced the means-tested FIS, the official Labour Party was united with outside observers in the view that even higher marginal tax rates would then face low-paid workers and their families. This was one main reason why Labour opposed the introduction of FIS in the first place.

Now the controversy is whether the poverty trap is getting worse or better, and indeed whether it still exists at all. In theory it is true that if a man earned an extra £1 a week in 1976 this could mean a loss of more than £1 to his family because of the poverty trap, ie extra payments due and the benefits withdrawn, but in practice how many poor families do still face this and how much of the problem has been solved by changes in the tax threshold or by benefits which run for a full year irrespective of pay rises?

The debate is certainly characterised by firm pronouncements from each side. The government view is unambiguously that the poverty trap no longer presents a serious problem. In reply to a parliamentary question in November 1975 the answer was that 'steps already taken ensure that the effects of the poverty trap are very limited in practice' (*Hansard* 4 November 1975).

On the empirical side a major official study of a sample of more than 600 two-parent families in receipt of FIS was published in 1975 (Department of Health and Social Security 1975). This report devoted a complete chapter to the poverty trap and to its effects on the families in the survey; in particular it tried to examine 'the true effect of interacting means tests', saying that other commentators 'have sometimes oversimplified the problem by ignoring the fact that some income-tested benefits can take a considerable period to react to a change in income, during which time other factors may change'. Mr Howell MP, however, writing in December 1975, claimed that the poverty trap 'now ensnares a growing number of families' (Howell 1975). Pond and Ward, looking at the likely effect of the £6 pay limit on the living standards of the poor, concluded that, of those workers who receive the full £6 earnings increase, 'most of these families will be only a few pence better off after an increase of that size, and many will find themselves worse off than before. The present structure of taxes and means-tested benefits ensures that the heaviest burden will be shouldered by those least able to bear it' (Pond and Ward 1975).

I cannot say for certain who was right because it would require evidence from representative sample surveys carried out in 1975 to say how many families were that year affected by the poverty trap and by how much. The Low Pay Unit, who carried out ·a survey of 110 agricultural workers in 1975, pointed out that 'those caught in the poverty trap are only too well aware of how they are affected', and they found that 25 out of the 94 who were receiving FIS were trapped in this way. But I could not 'gross up' this figure to give an overall answer. The DHSS study of 614 two-parent families receiving FIS was a more representative sample, though it excluded one-parent families and the survey was in any case carried out in 1972. I can, however, do exercises similar to those I did last year by making various assumptions about increases in gross pay between October 1974 and October 1975 and, after allowing for changes in taxes and eligibility levels for benefits, comparing the outcomes. I shall therefore try to make some kind of general assessment on the effects of the poverty trap in 1975 in the next section on living standards.

Changes in living standards

In 1975 the debate on changing living standards and in particular whether the poor are getting poorer or less poor took on a new dimension. Mr Healey argued, in a published letter to Frank Field *(Guardian* 7 June 1975), that, contrary to the impression given in CPAG's post-Budget memorandum and in its new memorandum published on 4 June (Child Poverty Action Group 1975a and 1975b), the government had successfully protected the living standards of poorer families and that indeed in many cases poorer families had actually become better off, improving their living standards at a time of exceptional economic difficulty. What the Chancellor's tables actually showed, however, as CPAG were quick to point out was that 'if workers had broken the social contract' and received pay increases equal to the average level of settlements from

Table 3.2 Change in real disposable resources October 1974 – October 1975

	Social Contract pay rise 26% increase in gross earnings			National average pay rise 28% increase in gross earnings		
	Take home pay %	Money disposable income %	Real disposable resources %	Take home pay %	Money disposable income %	Real disposable resources %
Low-paid worker (£29.30 a week in 1974)						
Single Person	21.8	22.8	-3.6	23.5	24.9	-1.5
Couple and 1 child	21.0	16.8	-9.4	22.4	16.8	-9.4
Couple and 4 children	20.7	17.0	-9.0	21.9	16.4	-9.6
Average worker (£43.80 a week in 1974)						
Single person	21.8	22.5	-4.4	23.2	24.1	-2.8
Couple and 1 child	21.2	21.8	-4.5	22.5	23.4	-2.9
Couple and 4 children	21.5	18.2	-7.7	22.6	19.0	-6.9
Affluent worker (£68.80 a week in 1974)						
Single person	22.8	23.3	-3.7	24.9	25.6	-1.4
Couple and 1 child	22.3	22.8	-3.3	24.3	25.0	-1.1
Couple and 4 children	22.4	23.1	-2.7	24.2	25.0	-0.8

March 1974 to March 1975 then they had 'experienced a real increase in their net disposable income' by 60p a week for the one-child family and by 4p a week for the three-child family. However, low-paid workers who had struck settlements within the social contract 'are now worse off in real terms' (*Guardian* 10 June 1975).

In Table 3.2 I look, amongst other things, at whether these conclusions still hold for the period October 1974 to October 1975, ie whether sticking to the social contract meant losing out in real terms, whereas getting pay rises in line with everyone else meant getting ahead.

My starting point is the low-paid worker on £29.30 a week in 1974, which is two-thirds of that of the average worker on £43.80. The affluent worker on £68.80 a week received pay of 1½ times the average. Receiving a pay increase in line with the cost of living meant a 26% rise from October 1974 to October 1975. On this basis the low-paid worker would have been on £36.90 a week, the average worker on £55.20 and the affluent on £86.70 in 1975. Getting increases in line with everyone else's earnings meant, as we saw in the last chapter, slightly more than this – a 28% increase in earnings in 1974-75. On this basis the low-paid worker would have been on £37.50 a week, the average on £55.90 and the affluent on £88.20.

The first and fourth columns of Table 3.2 show what the 26% and 28% gross pay increases meant in terms of take-home pay, by which I mean after taking account of income tax, national insurance contributions and family allowances where applicable. On the last of these, the increases to £1.50 per child for the second and subsequent children could have helped improve the position of some families relative to single persons and childless couples, but the gains on this score were to a large extent offset by the decline in the value of the child tax allowances. The outcome is that for the low-paid worker, despite equal increases in gross pay, the couple with four children fared worse in terms of increases in take-home pay than the couple with one child, who in turn did less well than the single person. Single person households also fared best at the level of the average and affluent workers.

In his April Budget Mr Healey, after imposing his 'inflation surcharge', warned that 'similar measures may be necessary in the future if wage settlements are not kept under better control'.

Different measures which did not penalise families with children would perhaps be more appropriate.

To get at money disposable income I take account of housing costs, rent and rate rebates and family income supplement where appropriate. On housing I make the same assumptions as did the government in a written answer to a parliamentary question in November 1975 (*Hansard* 10 November 1975). This is that all the workers are tenants, and that rent and rates are the same at each income level. Of course in any comprehensive analysis I would need to look at owner occupiers too, perhaps differentiating between those who had just taken out a mortgage and those who had almost paid theirs off, and I would want to allow for differential housing expenditure at different income levels. But, as with the government's own analysis, my purpose here is merely illustrative, so the government's assumptions will do. This means that for a single person, rent (before rebates, if any) was £3.61 and rates (likewise unrebated) £1.37 in 1975; for a married couple and one child rent was £4.13 and rates £1.58; and for a married couple and four children rent was £4.94 and rates £1.88. I assume that rents increased by 50p to 60p for October 1974 to October 1975 and rates by 25p to 35p. The former was in line with what was allowed following the replacement of the rent freeze by phased-in rent increases, and the latter with average rate increases for local authority dwellings in England and Wales. I also assume that all means-tested benefits are claimed where eligible.

After taking account of all these factors the single person still comes out best at all income levels and irrespective of whether he stuck to the social contract or broke it. If he was a worker earning low pay or average earnings he was doing even better here relative to families with children than he was when only take-home pay was taken into account. In part this outcome is the result of the assumptions I made about housing costs and perhaps the burden of these will alter soon. The Layfield Committee on the financing of local government is reporting in 1976 and it is likely that major changes will be recommended on local rates. The outcome also points, however, to the need for rebates of rent and rates, or whatever other form of housing allowances are decided on, to take more account than hitherto of how families with children are faring as against single persons.

Finally to get at real disposable resources I had, as in previous years, to construct special price indices for households of different types and at different income levels. I did this on the basis of their different expenditure patterns as revealed by the 1974 Family Expenditure Survey (the latest available at the time of writing), and weighted by the respective price increases for each of the broad commodity groups which make up the official retail price index.

The final figures, on changes in living standards, are given in the third and last columns of Table 3.2. From this it can be seen that no one maintained their 1974 position, irrespective of whether they kept to the social contract or broke it. This is because, as I showed in the previous chapter, the gap between earnings and prices was exceptionally wide for the period covered by CPAG and Mr Healey, and it grew much narrower as the full data for the first phase of the social contract became available.

Table 3.2 also shows that there was one exception to the rule that those who kept to the contract did worse than those who broke it, and that was the low-paid worker with four children. He was worse off with a 28% increase in earnings than with a 26% one. This was because of the poverty trap. The withdrawal of means-tested benefits such as rent and rate rebate and FIS, coupled with extra income tax and national insurance contributions meant that more than £1 was lost for the extra £1 earned.

So far I have concentrated on the comparative fortunes of those who stuck to or broke the social contract, and on horizontal equity ie families with children compared to single persons at each income level. Now I want to focus on vertical equity ie lower compared with higher income groups. My final point on Table 3.2 therefore is that, among the couples with one child and the families with four children, the affluent worker comes out better than the average worker, who in turn does better than the low-paid. This is despite the assumption that they all got equal percentage increases in gross pay.

Living standards on alternative assumptions

The monitoring of overall changes in living standards has become more sophisticated since the first *Poverty Report* was published two years ago. The organisation Labour Research in

Table 3.3 Changes in real disposable resources October 1974 – October 1975 on alternative assumptions about gross pay and employment opportunities

	Take home pay %	£6 increase in gross earnings				Unemployed in October 1975	
		Money disposable income %	Real disposable resources %			Money disposable income %	Real disposable resources %
Low-paid worker (£29.30 a week in 1974)							
Single person	16.9	16.6	– 9.8			– 37%	– 63%
Couple and 4 children	17.6	18.2	– 7.8			– 3%	– 29%
Average worker (£43.80 a week in 1974)							
Single person	8.6	7.1	– 19.8			3%	– 23%
Couple and 4 children	11.4	10.4	– 15.5			– 16%	– 42%
Affluent worker (£68.80 a week in 1974)							
Single person	4.3	3.0	– 24.0			17%	– 9%
Couple and 4 children	8.2	7.1	– 18.7			13%	– 13%

1975 made the point that the timing of particular pay settlements is relevant (Labour Research 1975). I usually look at changes between October in one year and October in the next, but between October 1974 and October 1975 the date at which people received increases made a lot of difference to them. If it was at the beginning of the year and was within the social contract guidelines they would have kept up with the cost of living. If it came in August or September 1975 they would have received only £6 a week more, much less than the then current rate of inflation. Mr Healey himself stressed that the position of individual families would vary depending 'on the date' as well as the 'size of pay increase'. In past years I have not taken account of this aspect, but I try to do so this year in Table 3.3.

Of course the £6 increase is supposed to cover the period 1975-76, during which it is hoped that the rate of inflation will be down to an annual rate of 10% or less; but workers in the glass industry, for example, who settled for £6 in August 1975 had to set it against an annual rate of inflation 25%. Moreover, the relative effects on workers at different income levels can be examined independently of the rate of inflation and it is this that I want to look at too.

The first three columns of Table 3.3, constructed in the same way as in Table 3.2, show the outcome. From this it can be seen that with £6 a week the low-paid workers fare best and the affluent worst, and families with four children do better than single persons. In these respects, this is in my opinion a much better outcome than that of Table 3.2.

Living standards of the poor are however still declining and, in the absence of further policy changes, likely to continue to do so throughout the duration of the £6 pay limit policy. The government admits that workers in general are expected to take their cut in living standards, but has pledged itself to safeguard the standards of the poorest. It will need to do still more for the poor if this pledge is to become a reality.

A second cause for modifying my procedure is the large increase in unemployment. The financial problems and provisions for the unemployed are discussed in more detail in the next chapter, but in a period of high unemployment like the present it would seem a mistake to confine attention solely to low-paid workers in full-time work throughout the year. While recognising that I cannot consider all the subtleties, such as the influence of short-time working, I also look in Table 3.3 at year-on-year changes for workers who lost their jobs in 1975.

When a worker first loses his job he may be entitled to redundancy payments, earnings-related supplements and tax rebates, all of which could soften the blow. After a few months, however, the tax rebate will run out; after six, so will the earnings-related benefit; after 12 flat-rate national insurance unemployment benefit will be exhausted and from then on the family will have to rely on the ordinary rate of supplementary benefit. In the final two columns of Table 3.3 the formerly low-paid worker who became unemployed is assumed to be on supplementary benefit in October 1975. The previously average and affluent workers are assumed to be getting earnings-related national insurance benefit but not tax rebates. All experience a drop in living standards as a result of losing their jobs, with the low-paid and average workers particularly hard hit.

Conclusions

In this chapter and the previous one I have been trying to trace changes in living standards from one year to the next. My conclusions this year, perhaps even more than usual, have to be hedged with qualifications. On one thing however we can be sure. Living standards for all groups, including the low paid, fell between October 1974 and October 1975. Even if the low paid got exceptionally large pay increases they were still caught in the poverty trap, and for others the pay rises required to maintain real disposable resources were far outside the reach of most. If the head of a poor or average family lost his job and could not get another, then after a while they were the worst off of all.

The £6 a week pay policy is unlikely to reverse this trend of falling living standards for the period October 1975 to October 1976, and new initiatives are needed if the poor are to be protected. The £6 policy has, however, at least helped ensure that the inflation is more fairly shared and that the biggest burdens rest on the broadest backs. This is the exact opposite to what occurred with the earlier policy of general cost of living increases.

On the more specific issues touched on in the earlier parts of this chapter, I would add these comments. First, the income tax system seems to be in urgent need of reform. Tax burdens for the low paid continue to rise, and the after-tax distribution of income looks very similar to the pre-tax one. National insurance contributions only add to the problems. A more overall view of objectives and alternative methods of achieving them is clearly called for. This should take account of income maintenance and income tax at the same time. Only in this way will the poverty trap be eliminated.

Secondly, I would underline the obvious point that prices count as well as incomes. Despite the arguments against subsidies they do have two advantages. They benefit all of the poor, whereas means-tested benefits only go to those who claim, and they help housewives directly.

Finally, I have concentrated on living standards as measured by changing pay packets. For many, especially those not at work but others as well, it is the size of the social wage that counts most. In the next chapter I look at inflation and the social wage.

References

Age Concern (1974) *Shopping for Food*, Age Concern

M. Brown and S. Winyard (1975) *Low Pay on the Farm*, Low Pay Pamphlet 3, Low Pay Unit

Child Poverty Action Group (1975a) *Reducing the Poor's Living Standards at a Stroke*, Child Poverty Action Group

Child Poverty Action Group (1975b) *Back to the Thirties for the Poor? Report number 1 on the Living Standards of the Poor in 1975*, Child Poverty Action Group

Department of Employment (1975a) *The Unstatistical Reader's Guide to the Retail Price Index*, Department of Employment Gazette, October 1975, HMSO

Department of Employment (1975b) *How the Prices Barometer Works*, DE News no. 25, Department of Employment

Department of Health and Social Security (1975) *Two-Parent Families in Receipt of Family Income Supplement*, Statistical and Research Series Report no. 9, HMSO

R. Howell (1975) *Low Pay and Taxation* Low Pay Paper no. 8, Low Pay Unit

Labour Research (1975) *Report for October 1975*, Labour Research

T. Liesner and M. King (eds) (1975) *Indexing for Inflation*, Institute for Fiscal Studies, Heinemann

National Consumer Council (1975) *For Richer for Poorer: The Problems Facing Low Income Consumers*, National Consumer Council

C. Pond (1975) *Inflation and Low Wage Earners*, Low Pay Bulletin no. 5, Low Pay Unit

C. Pond and S. Ward (1975) *The £6 Trap*, Low Pay Unit Paper no. 6, Low Pay
    Unit
Royal Commission on the Distribution of Income and Wealth (1975) *Report
    No 1: Initial Report on the Standing Reference*, Cmnd 6171 July 1975, HMSO
P. Townsend *et al*. (1975) *Inflation and Low Incomes*, Fabian research series 322,
    Fabian Society

This chapter is about three things – the so-called social wage, the proposed cuts in public spending and the changing circumstances of those who depend on social security benefits. The plight of the unemployed, whose ranks have been swelling, demands special attention.

4 Inflation and the social wage

CHRIS TRINDER

In the last chapter I looked at the effect on personal incomes of income tax, national insurance, local rates and taxes on spending. These deductions, along with other taxes such as those on companies and capital, can also be seen as sources of public revenue. In this chapter I examine the way in which the government spends part of the money it collects. The subject is the so-called 'second wage': the social wage provided by the government as distinct from the wage paid by employers.

Raising and spending public revenue of course affects other things besides incomes. The balance of the nation's resources between consumption and saving, for example, will be altered to the extent that the person or company paying taxes pays them out of savings and the recipient of the social wage spends them. The distributional effects are, however, also important, and I focus on these in this chapter.

The concept of a social wage got a new lease of life in 1975 and I begin by examining its aggregate changes and how inflation affected it. I then turn to the more familiar ground of previous *Poverty Reports* and, in terms of broad categories of people, examine who gets how much from social security and what was happening to the value of such payments in 1975. This year I give special attention to the financial position of the unemployed who, after retirement pensioners, were in 1975 the second largest group of recipients of social security. In the final part I look at the public expenditure cuts.

Public spending on the social wage
Selling 'public expenditure' became a major activity of Labour politicians in the first part of 1975. Barbara Castle put the case like this

> The most important part of the standard of living of most of us depends on the great complex of services we call 'public expenditure'. They are not only the key to the quality of life; they are the key to equality . . . The great advances . . . have come . . . from better education, better health services, better housing and better care of the old, the disabled and the handicapped in life.

The social wage constitutes 60% of total public expenditure. Excluded are, for example, defence expenditure and the National Enterprise Board. Mrs Castle, given the prominent contribution of her department, was not surprisingly particularly keen to stress the importance of the social wage (*Financial Times* 8 July 1975), arguing that 'the taxman is the Robin Hood of our time, taking from those who can afford it the means whereby we can pay every worker the wage that really matters, the social wage'.

It was not just politicians who caught on to the idea. The Retail Price Index Advisory Committee, reporting in February 1975, recommended that further consideration should be given to the construction of 'a more elaborate index which would take account of elements of social spending and subventions of income of all kinds, in other words an index of what is sometimes described as the "social wage".' As a result the government set up an inter-departmental committee called Joint Action on Social Policy to examine this. Their first report, published later in 1975, reaffirmed the importance of the social wage and the value of a special index (Central Review Staff 1975).

The social wage, according to Mr Healey in his Budget speech (15 April 1975), was in 1975 worth the equivalent of £1,000 for every adult member of the working population in the United Kingdom. Exactly how this total was arrived at was not revealed at the time, but subsequently (*Hansard* 22 April 1975) the government gave the following breakdown:

	£
Social security	270
Education, libraries etc	210
Health and personal social services	180
Housing	160
Other environmental services	70
Law and order	50
Food, nationalised industries price restraint and main transport subsidies	60

Total £1,000

From this it is clear that, apart from social security which is discussed in this chapter, the largest items are health, housing and education which are dealt with respectively in Chapters 6, 7 and 8. Of course not everyone receives this 'average' package of services, and other chapters look at who actually gets what. In Chapter 6, for example, Phyllis Willmott presents some individual case studies of families living in Lambeth in 1975.

The statement that led to most discussion was one made by Mr Healey in his April Budget: he asserted that the 'social wage has been increasing very much faster than ordinary wages – much faster than prices too'. Even after taking account of the general level of inflation, it was supposed to have risen by 7% from 1972-73 to 1973-74 and by 12% from 1973-74 to 1974-75. The TUC were quick to qualify this by correctly pointing out that the costs involved in providing it, like labour costs and items such as drugs which rose rapidly in price, had been hit harder than average by inflation and that it 'requires growing amounts of resources in inflationary conditions such as the present' merely to maintain existing levels of services. Mr Healey's statement also needs to be qualified by taking into account the increased scope which the social wage has to cover:

> The social wage is paid mainly for the benefit of that greater half of the population that does not receive a working wage or salary . . . wage earners are already outnumbered by the total of dependent children, elderly persons, sick or disabled persons, mothers rearing children, and unemployed . . . later school leaving and earlier retirement are likely to reduce still further the proportion of wage-earners in the population during the coming years and increase further the importance of the social wage (Wynn 1971).

Social security expenditure, which represents 27% of the total social wage, increased by 110% in cash terms – 22% after taking account of the general rise in prices – between 1971-72 and 1975-76. This was roughly in line with the increase in the social wage as a whole. Some components such as education rose more, and others like personal social services less (Chancellor of the Exchequer 1975). For social security, however, as for other elements, there were important reasons why these figures overstated the true expansion of services. Several factors which contributed to the growth of social security spending cannot be seen as reducing poverty (Atkinson 1972).

Unemployment provides one example. In Britain, as elsewhere, it has been increasing rapidly and now stands at more than one million, almost 5% of the labour force. Increased social security expenditure caused by more people losing their jobs hardly represents an advance. The increase in the number of elderly people is also relevant. It is officially estimated that there will be 500,000 more retirement pensioners in 1978-79 than there were in 1973-74 even if the retirement age remains as it is at 65 for men and 60 for women. In France, pressure to make it 60 for all looks like succeeding. If this happens in Britain too then each year another £1,500 million or so would have to be found to meet the cost of providing pensions for the extra 1½ million pensioners (*Hansard* 4 November 1975).

Nevertheless, during the past 20 years the social wage as a whole, and social security expenditure to the extent that it moved in step, has increased as a proportion of the consumption on which people themselves spend and only part of this can be accounted for by the qualifications just outlined. The total social wage rose as a proportion of private consumption from a third in the early 1950s (33% in 1955) to two-fifths in the early 1960s (40% in 1963) to a half in the late 1960s (53% in 1969) to three-fifths in the early 1970s (59% in 1973) (*Hansard* 15 July 1975).

The abolition of poverty

Despite the increase in the total size of the social wage, poverty has certainly not been abolished. In Chapters 10 and 11, as in earlier *Poverty Reports,* 120% of supplementary benefit (SB) level has been taken as the poverty line. But even if poverty is defined more stringently than this – as those with income from all sources, including social security benefits, actually below supplementary benefit level – there were over one million people in poverty in December 1974.

Table 4.1, supplied by the Department of Health and Social Security, shows the number of families, and of people, who in December 1974 had incomes less than 120% of SB level (the justification for using this definition is explained in Chapter II). The table also breaks the total down into those above SB but within 20% of it, those getting SB and those with income below SB but not receiving it.

The table shows that 2½ million families were dependent on SB and 1¼ million had incomes within 20% above it. The majority of these were retired. Beveridge hoped that SB would form a minor part of the system of social security, a safety net for those without other forms of support. This has not happened. For old people, the main reason is that the national insurance retirement pension is below SB level so that many retired people have to claim both (Lister 1975).

Of the 920,000 families with incomes below SB level, 450,000 were over pensionable age. This was usually because they were not claiming the SB to which they were entitled. The other 470,000 were, however, people under pensionable age. With them, the explanation was not simply that they did not take up their full entitlement of means-tested benefits. Many had no automatic right to have their income raised to SB level. One such category of people in December 1974, although not now, was those who were wage-stopped ie people who had their SB reduced when unemployed because they earned low wages when at work. The wage stop, affecting some 30,000 families, was abolished in 1975 – a welcome reform. One kind of family still ineligible for SB is that whose head is in full-time work but earns low pay. He can get means-tested family income supplement but this guarantees only half the gap between low pay and prescribed income levels.

Social security benefits and what they buy

How did the main social security benefits change in value during 1975? In November new rates were introduced, following an earlier increase in April, and the government made much of the argument that benefit levels were in 1975 increasing much faster than both prices and earnings (*Hansard* 27

Table 4.1 Families with low net resources in Great Britain, December 1974

	Below SB and not receiving it		Receiving SB		Above SB but within 20% of it		120% of SB or less	
	Families (thousands)	Persons in these families (thousands)	Families (thousands)	Persons in these families (thousands)	Families (thousands)	Persons in these families (thousands)	Families (thousands)	Persons in these families (thousands)
1 *Over pensionable age* (60 for women, 65 for men)	450	550	1,810	2,130	1,030	1,360	3,280	4,040
2 *Under pensionable age* Family head or single person:								
normally in full-time work	130	360	–	–	140	520	270	890
sick or disabled for more than three months	20	60	280	420	30	90	330	570
unemployed for more than three months	40	90	140	360	30	60	210	510
others	280	350	300	820	70	120	650	1,300
Total under pensionable age	470	850	720	1,600	270	800	1,460	3,250
3 *Total of 1 and 2*	920	1,410	2,530	3,730	1,300	2,160	4,740	7,300

November 1975). They claimed that national insurance retirement pensions, for example, were 33% higher in November 1975 than in November 1974 whereas prices were up by only 25%. Part of the explanation, however, is that November 1975 was a month when benefits were increased whereas November 1974 was not. If the government had set October 1975, the month before the benefits were increased, against October 1974, the comparison would have suggested that there had been a dramatic 10% fall in living standards. The choice of dates is thus crucial to the exercise. To get over this problem what I did last year was to compare only months when the benefits were increased, and I do this again here in Table 4.2

I should first explain how the increases are calculated. In last year's *Poverty Report* I explained that the April 1975 rises announced before the end of 1974 were decided by reference to the increase in the monthly index of earnings between November 1973 and August 1974, roughly 16%, and prices over the same period, which increased by 13%. Long term national insurance eg retirement pensions and supplementary benefit rates were increased in line with the former, and short term ones eg sickness benefit in line with the latter. To decide the increases for November 1975 the same procedure was adopted, only this time it was the prices and earnings index between August 1974 and March 1975 that counted. Over that period earnings increased by 14½% and prices by 13½% and this roughly determined the respective increases in long and short term benefits from November 1975.

Originally, the benefit increases which in fact came in November were announced for a month later, December. The change of date, Barbara Castle argued, was so as to provide extra help for the poor. How far this was really the reason we do not know, but it is possible that she belatedly realised that to increase benefits in line with an eight month rise in the Retail Price Index would cover the period August 1974 (the last month used for calculating the previous increases) to April 1975. April is usually the month when prices increase most rapidly because local authority rate increases, water charges, the effects of the Budget and other substantial price rises all come at that time. April 1975 was no exception. Sticking to the original plan would have meant that short term benefits would

Table 4.2 Changes in standard of living of pensioners, the unemployed and one-parent families 1974-75

	July 1974 – April 1975		April 1975 – November 1975		July 1974 – November 1975	
	Increase in disposable money resources	Increase in purchasing power after taking account of inflation	Increase in disposable money resources	Increase in purchasing power after taking account of inflation	Increase in disposable money resources	Increase in purchasing power after taking account of inflation
	%	%	%	%	%	%
Unemployed man, wife and 2 children claiming SB	14.3	– 3.4	13.3	1.7	29.5	– 1.9
Retirement pensioner couple	15.6	– 2.1	14.6	3.0	32.5	1.1
One-parent family and 1 child claiming SB for more than two years	15.2	– 2.5	13.9	2.3	31.3	0
One-parent family and 1 child claiming SB for less than two years	14.2	– 3.5	13.5	1.9	29.6	– 1.8

Note: The increases in the first two and last two columns are expressed as percentages of the levels of benefit existing in July 1974. Those in the middle two columns are in relation to the higher rates in operation in April 1975. Only if all had been expressed in terms of July 1974 benefits would the numbers for July 1974 – November 1975 equal the sum of the other two periods.

have had to go up by 17½% in December. Increasing them in November meant that Barbara Castle had to put them up by only 13½%.

As long as the same method is used for determining future increases in benefit, then the April price rises will count next time, but the government will still have gained by paying 13½% rather than 17½% each month from December 1975 until the next increase. It is true that 13½% extra was paid in November compared to what would have been the rate then if the benefits had not been increased until December, but by March 1975 this had been more than offset by the 4% saving in each of four succeeding months, and each month from then on lost the poor that much more. Increasing benefits in November 1975 rather than December turned out to be a very effective way of reducing public expenditure.

Barbara Castle could argue that, despite what I have said about the effects of her bringing forward the increases to November, the 13½% increases in the short term rates were still sufficient to more than compensate for the actual rise in prices between April and November 1975. The third and fourth columns of Table 4.2 confirm that this was so for all categories of recipient. This was bound to happen, however, because the rate of inflation was decelerating during that period and the pension rises were calculated on the past increases in earnings and prices. The first and second columns of Table 4.2 which cover the period when inflation was accelerating, July 1974 to April 1975, show that the exact opposite occurred then. No group of recipients had a pension rise in April 1975 which compensated for the actual rise in prices from July 1974.

I should perhaps say something about the fact that the worst off group of recipients over the July 1974 to April 1975 period is the one-parent family who, because they have been drawing SB for less than two years, are entitled to only the ordinary rate, whereas over the April 1975 to November 1975 period the family of the unemployed man, also entitled to only the ordinary rate of SB, did least well. The paradox is explained by the fact that over the July 1974 to April 1975 period the SB rate for a single householder (in this case the lone parent) rose marginally less fast than that for the married couple, but over the April 1975 to November 1975 period it was the other way round.

In terms of my main concern about the best choice of dates

for the assessment of changes in living standards, it is perhaps fairest to put both the July 1974 to April 1975 and April 1975 to November 1975 periods together. This avoids conditions particularly favourable or particularly unfavourable for the comparison. The change in living standards for the four groups of recipients over the whole period July 1974 to November 1975 is shown in the last two columns of Table 4.2. From this it can be seen that, as in last year's *Poverty Report,* recipients on the long term rate were protected against inflation while those on the ordinary rate, which includes both lone parents in receipt of SB for less than two years and the unemployed however long they were out of work, were not.

There was in 1975 much confusion about the living standards of the unemployed. In the *Financial Times* in July Sam Brittan wrote about 'workers who can take home more money when jobless' and showed that a worker with two children earning £55 per week gross and having a disposable income of £34.26. after tax and national insurance contributions would from November 1975 be receiving £34.93 including getting his tax rebate and earnings-related unemployment benefit. He concluded 'that the more generous treatment of people with a good earnings record in transition between jobs is one of the reasons why unemployment now fluctuates around a higher level than in the early 1960s'.

But what is it like to have a poor earnings record and be out of work for a long time? Sinfield (1975) pointed out that over half the unemployed registered for work at any one of the quarterly counts in 1975 were not receiving any national insurance unemployment benefit at all, let alone the earnings-related supplement, and that this proportion was rising. It would have been even greater if included in the total were those looking for work but not registered; this was equivalent at the time of the 1971 General Household Survey to a third of the registered unemployed.

For many who were unemployed but not receiving national insurance benefit, the explanation was that they had been unemployed for more than 12 months or had experienced recurrent unemployment, and had thereby exhausted their entitlement. For them supplementary benefit at the ordinary rate (ie not the long term) was the sole source of support. Table 4.2 shows the percentage changes in the value of this benefit, but it is perhaps worth putting them in absolute terms too. For a husband, wife and two children aged seven and eight, this benefit was, at November 1975 prices, worth £25.55 a week in July 1974 and £25.25 in November 1975. Despite the growth in total national income, there has been no increase in the real value of this benefit over the ten years since 1966. In the ten years before that, national assistance, as it was then called, rose 75% or so in value. The plight of the long-term unemployed has never been good, but in recent years they have in many ways been discriminated against even more than in the past.

Some benefits are not tied to either prices or earnings. Of these, earnings and capital disregards (the amounts ignored when calculating entitlement to SB) were increased faster than were both in 1975. The capital disregard went up by 50% to £1,200 and the earnings one doubled from £1 to £2 for a claimant required to register for work and by £2 to £4 for one who is not. These increases were, however, the first since 1966 and, large as they were, were not sufficient to restore their purchasing power since then. Other items like the lump sum maternity grant and the maximum death grant remained unchanged in 1975 at £25 and £30 respectively, and so did the 25p extra for the over-80s, which has remained at that amount since 1971. In 1975 the real value of all these items was considerably reduced.

Public expenditure cuts

In the late 1970s the social wage will certainly not continue to grow as before. Public expenditure estimates for 1975-76 show an expected nil rate of increase after taking account of inflation. Cuts proposed in 1975 for 1976-77 lop £1,100 million off previously planned programmes and about £500 million of this will fall on the social wage. As a result it is bound to decline in value compared to previous years (*Hansard* 5 November 1975). The axe will fall on the social wage items in the following way:

Public Expenditure Cuts 1976-77

£million (1975 prices)

Social security	0
Housing	129
Law and order	33
Health and personal social services	98
Education and libraries	110
Other environmental services	119
	489

The one item in the social wage that looks as though it will not be cut back is social security. The government is now pledged by law to raise short term benefits in line with prices, and long term in line with average earnings or prices. It would be impossible to go back on this except by changing the law. We have seen earlier, however, that there are good reasons, such as unexpectedly high unemployment levels, why the government may need more money than budgeted for merely to meet this commitment. By providing no guarantee of when the increases are to be granted, the government have left themselves at least one way out. In 1975 Barbara Castle said that Labour were increasing benefits twice a year (in fact they went up in April 1975 eight months after the previous increase and in November 1975 seven months later and would have to go up again in April 1976 for a six-monthly pattern) and that she wanted to get back to once-a-year increases as soon as possible. Returning to annual reviews of benefit levels would mean that smaller rates would be payable for more months and the government could in this way cut public expenditure without welshing on their pledge to increase benefits in line with prices or earnings.

It is not only by adjusting the time period that money could be saved on social security spending. Another key element is the index adopted for measuring the rises in earnings and prices as a basis for calculating increases. There are longer term proposals for changing the whole basis of the index, but apart from that the government has started publishing official forecasts of expected price and wage movements for future months. If these were adopted as the basis for calculating the pension increases and they showed, as they are likely to do, smaller increases than the actual past wage and price rises which would otherwise have been used, then pensioners would lose out as a result of the changeover, and the government would save money.

So far I have concentrated on ways in which public expenditure might be reduced, but which I think should not be adopted. As an alternative, and a good one in my opinion, the government could consider increasing some forms of taxation. Mr Healey argued in the debate on the Queen's speech in November that 'there is little scope for increasing taxation without unacceptable consequences in other areas of the economy' and that even 'if all income after tax above £6,000 a year were completely confiscated the additional yield would be only £450 million' (*Hansard* 25 November 1975). But, in addition to the possibility of abolishing the ceiling on national insurance contributions, mentioned in the last chapter, there does seem scope for cuts in certain tax allowances, and the sums involved could be much more than £450 million. Field and Meacher (1975) in their evidence to the expenditure committee inquiring into the financing of public expenditure cited, for example, income tax reliefs on mortgage interest, life assurance premiums, employers' and employees' contributions to occupational pension schemes and annuities as possible candidates for revision. It would seem reasonable to consider withdrawing these tax allowances as well as, and to some extent instead of, cutting public spending.

Conclusion

In this chapter I have been trying to say who gets what in wages from the state, and whether the poorest have been getting more in 1975. The findings are not encouraging. Compared with July 1974 the increases in benefits in November 1975 did not maintain living standards for all groups of recipient. Those dependent on the ordinary rate of supplementary benefit, which includes large numbers of the long term unemployed, did particularly badly. If one takes account of the decision not to pay £10 Christmas bonuses this year – worth, for a married couple, the equivalent of 40p a week throughout the year – then even those on the long term rates lost out. The living standards of the poorest need to be protected much more effectively than they are being at present.

For those on the lowest incomes it is not enough simply to stop them becoming even worse off. A big shift upwards is required too. In the immediate future, with the present economic difficulties, there are unlikely to be major changes in policy to achieve this, though more determined efforts could be made by the Supplementary Benefits Commission under their new Chairman, David Donnison, to help those entitled to benefits, but not receiving them to get all they should. By this I mean not just SB, which many, especially the old, still do not claim, but also heating allowances, exceptional circumstances additions and exceptional needs payments, for which take up is also very low. In the longer term, when resources permit, these means-tested benefits should be phased out, perhaps along the lines suggested by Lister (1975), by for example paying the national insurance unemployment benefit and retirement pensions at higher rates than SB and making eligibility for them easier and last longer.

Finally, the public expenditure cuts should come only after full consideration of their distributional implications. This requires finding out much more than we have about how much benefit the poor derive from the different services relative to the rest of us. Also the cuts should be decided within the widest possible terms of reference. The costs simply of maintaining existing levels of provision should be more fully appreciated and the possibility of withdrawing certain tax allowances examined very carefully.

References

A.B. Atkinson (1972) 'Inequality and social security', Bosanquet and Townsend (eds) *Labour and Inequality*, Fabian Society

Central Staff Review (1975) *Joint Framework for Social Policy*, HMSO

Chancellor of the Exchequer (1975) *Public Expenditure 1978-79* Cmnd 5879, HMSO

F. Field and M. Meacher (1975) *The Changing Burden of Taxation* Evidence to Expenditure Committee on the Financing of Public Expenditure

R. Lister (1975) *Social Security: The Case for Reform* Child Poverty Action Group no. 22

Retail Prices Advisory Committee (1975) *Housing and Related Matters on the Retail Price Index*, Cmnd 5905, HMSO

A. Sinfield (1975) 'Benefits and the unemployed', *Poverty* no. 32 Child Poverty Action Group

M. Wynn (1971) *Family Policy*, Penguin

*The main concern so far has been economic deprivation
in 1975. The government is planning a new scheme for
child benefits to be phased in over the next few years.
This scheme could have far-reaching consequences for
poor families.*

5 Child benefits

CHRIS TRINDER

This chapter takes a longer view of the circumstances of
families and of the Labour government's proposals for new
child benefits. In the late 1970s these will replace child tax
allowances, family allowances and other benefits for children
by one single tax-free cash payment. This change could be the
most important since the Beveridge Report laid the founda-
tions for the Welfare State in the 1940s.

I begin by looking at families compared with childless couples. I then examine the government's financial provisions for
children in families of different sizes and types and at different
income levels. The inconsistencies and anomalies revealed constitute a case for reform. In the third section I look at how
Labour's plans for new child benefits propose to remedy this,
and in the final one at reactions to them, including some of the
criticisms put forward by the Child Poverty Action Group
(CPAG).

Penalising families with children

Hardly any family to which a child is added can secure an
addition to income which comes anywhere near meeting the
cost of the child's subsistence. If a couple with an average
income had four children their standard of living in 1975 was
about half what it would have been without them. Because
some people never marry, or marry and have no children, not
all adults carry this responsibility for bringing up the next
generation. Because some couples' children have not yet been

born and others have already grown up, the proportion in any one year is even smaller; about three-quarters of the children are in one-fifth of all households. 40% of the children – those with two or more brothers and sisters – are at any one time in less than one-tenth of the households.

Family poverty is not, however, found only in families with many children. The *Circumstances of Families* inquiry into living standards in families receiving family allowances, ie those with two or more children, found that, among those with the father in full-time work, one-third of families with an income below the supplementary benefit level had only two children (Ministry of Social Security 1967). Large families are of course particularly vulnerable, but so are those with older children, who cost more to keep, and with very young children where the mother cannot go out to work.

At the outset, there are three general points about families with children compared with single person households and childless couples. The first concerns the relationship between tax and the family, the second the changes over time in the value of family allowances, and the third the cost of living.

The way in which tax burdens on the low paid have increased was shown in Chapter 3. Mr Healey admitted the point when in the debate on the Queen's speech he said that 'income tax is already bearing heavily not only on the average worker, but also the low paid' (*Hansard* 25 November 1975). What is less well known is the way families at all income levels have been particularly hard hit as compared with single people. The combined effect is that low-paid families with children have been hit hardest of all. It is perhaps worth illustrating this in more detail.

Table 5.1 shows, for various dates over the past 15 years, the level of income at which tax first becomes due, called the tax threshold, in relation to national average earnings. In the table the relationship that existed between the tax threshold and average earnings in 1961-62 has been set at 100. If it rose above 100 in some subsequent years, as happened for the single person, this meant that tax did not become due until a higher level of income was earned. Conversely when the number fell below 100 this meant that the family started to become liable for tax at a lower level of earnings.

Table 5.1 Tax threshold in relation to national average earnings for different types of family at various dates 1961-62 to 1975-76

Financial year	Single person	Married couple with one child	Married couple with four children
1961-62	100	100	100
1966-67	119	99	93
1970-71	127	91	77
1973-74	124	81	60
1974-75	108	76	57
1975-76	92	64	47

Table 5.1 shows that the tax threshold for a four-child family had by 1975-76 fallen to less than half of its 1961-62 value. This fall was much more severe than that experienced by single persons. In fact in 1975-76 things get steadily worse as one moves from one person households, to childless couples (not shown in the table), to small and then to large families. Mr Healey gave us some idea of the extent of the problem of falling tax thresholds when he said that 'there are substantial numbers whose earnings are below the supplementary level but who are being taxed on them. To keep them out of tax would require raising the basic rate of tax by 3p to 38p' (*Hansard* 25 November 1975).

Tax burdens depend not just on the level at which tax starts to become due but also on the rate of tax on each band of taxable income. In 1961-62 the first £60 of taxable income was charged at a rate of only $8\frac{3}{4}\%$ whereas in 1975-76 the rate was 35% right from the start. The overall effect of these combined changes was that the percentage of total income taken in tax from families with children has risen markedly in recent years.

For the couple with four children and average earnings it rose from nothing in 1965-66 to 7% in 1975-76. For the low-paid couple with one child (two-thirds of national average earnings each year) income tax as a percentage of total income rose from 1% in 1965-66 to 6% in 1970-71 to 10% in 1974-75 and 15% in 1975-76. In 1975-76 such a family was paying £6.39 a week in income tax.

At the same time as tax burdens have been increasing cash benefits have been declining. Family allowances have remained unaltered in cash terms for many years at a time, and their real value, after taking account of inflation, has been much reduced. Family allowances recommended by Beveridge should have been 40p per child. In fact they were implemented at 25p because it was assumed that the system of free school meals, milk and welfare foods would be extended. Again in 1968, announcing the increases then, the government said that much of the increase in family allowances from 50p (40p for the second child) to £1 (90p for the second child) was designed to compensate low-income families for the effects of devaluation, the increased price of school meals, the withdrawal of milk in secondary schools and other changes (Townsend 1972). One ought to bear in mind the influence of such factors when relating the level of family allowances to the movement of prices or of wages, but a straightforward comparison of this kind can still be useful. The Beveridge target of 40p per child would in 1948 have represented an allowance of 5.8% of average earnings for a two-child family. In fact, as mentioned earlier, the family allowance was set at 25p in that year, equal to 3.6% of average earnings. Since then family allowances at their highest point, in 1952, were 4.5% and at their lowest point, in 1974, 1.8%. In 1975, after Labour had increased the levels to £1.50 per eligible child, family allowances represented 2.4% of average earnings, below the proportion in 1948 and well below the Beveridge target.

So far I have concentrated on incomes but it is also important to take account of what money can buy. I do this in Table 5.2 which uses the period October 1970 to October 1973 as an example. The calculations are done in the same way as the cost of living indices presented in Chapter 3.

Table 5.2 Differential effects of inflation October 1970 – October 1973 (expressed in terms of average annual percentage retail price increases)

	Couple with four children	Couple with one child	Single person
Low-paid worker (²⁄₃ national average earnings)	% 10.6	% 10.3	% 10.0
Average worker	10.4	10.0	9.6
Affluent worker (1½ times national average earnings)	10.1	9.6	9.2

The table shows that over the period the cost of living at all three income levels rose faster for families with children than for single people and faster for large families than small. The low-paid family with four children fared worst (10.6% per year) and the affluent single worker best (9.2% per year).

As successive *Poverty Reports* have shown, the picture has changed since the period covered in Table 5.2. In terms of prices, families with children have not fared worse than others. This was primarily because of the Labour government's food subsidies, rent freeze and housing subsidies. In 1976, however, when steps are taken towards phasing out food and housing subsidies, the cost of living is likely to rise faster for families with children than for childless households.

Current provisions for children

Benefits for children come in cash and kind. Cash benefits are provided in four main ways: family allowances, child tax allowances, family income supplement and national insurance and/or supplementary benefit. Family allowances are a flat-rate universal benefit at a rate (since April 1975) of £1.50 per child payable for the second and subsequent children in a family. They are subject to income tax so that their value falls as household income rises; and since 1968 a 'clawback' procedure, reducing child tax allowances for each child on whom a family allowance is drawn, ensures that their after-tax value is even smaller for those on higher incomes. A two-child family, for example, can only gain the full £1.50 from the family allowance if its income is below £30 a week. If its income is higher than this they have to pay income tax on it, which at the standard rate of 35% reduces its value by 52½p. Their child tax allowance is reduced too so that to them the family allowance is worth only 62½p. For those liable to higher rates of income tax the amount is even smaller.

The child tax allowance in 1975 – £240 for a child under 11, £275 for one aged 11-16 and £305 for a person over 16 – is not usually thought of as the same thing as family allowance. It is obvious, however, that the two should be considered together. If a family is relieved of paying tax because of a tax allowance for a child then its standard of living is 'increased' in exactly the same way as if it received a direct cash payment through family allowances (Titmuss 1962). Child tax allowances, unlike family allowances, increase in value with the level of income. They are of no benefit whatever to households whose incomes are so low that they are not liable for tax. Conversely they are worth £17.55 a week to the family with four children with a taxable income of £20,000 a year earned income because each pound of tax allowance can be set against the 83p highest rate of tax.

Given these different effects of the interaction of family allowances and child tax allowances at different levels of income and for families of different sizes, it is, as Atkinson (1975) has argued, difficult to believe that the arrangements as they stand at present represent a carefully considered evaluation of needs.

A family's entitlement to any of the remaining forms of cash benefit for dependent children depends on whether the head of the household is in full-time work or on the level of income or both. Where he or she is not at work, say because of unemployment, sickness or widowhood, the family may receive national insurance child benefits or, failing that, supplementary allowances for children. National Insurance (NI) benefit is at higher rates for first children than for others, but if family allowances (payable only to second and subsequent children) are taken into account, then the level is the same for all children including the first. There is, however, a higher rate for children of recipients of long-term rates than short-term. The rates from November 1975 are set out below. It is important to note that there are no variations due to differences in the age of the child, which is how tax allowances differ. They also differ from family allowances in that the latter provide nothing for the first child.

National insurance benefit (including family allowance where applicable) for dependent children from November 1975

	Invalidity, widows and retirement pensions	Unemployed and sick
All children	£6.50	£3.50

Instead of (or sometimes in addition to) NI benefits, supplementary benefits (SB) may be paid. Although, as with NI benefits, there are both long and short-term SB rates for adults, this distinction does not apply to the children's rates. The size of the SB allowances, unlike NI ones, does however vary according to the age of the child. The SB rates for children, as from November 1975, are set out below:

Supplementary allowances for children from November 1975

Age of child	Allowance for children
16 and 17	£6.70
13 – 15	£5.60
11 and 12	£4.60
5 – 10	£3.75
0 – 4	£3.10

If the head of the household is in full-time work, but the family still has a low income it may be eligible for family income supplement (FIS). This is worth 50p for every £1 the family's total income falls below prescribed income limits, up to a maximum £7 for a one-child family plus 50p more for each extra child. Because FIS is a means-tested benefit its value falls sharply as income rises. For a four-child family the eligibility level was in December 1975 £42 a week, so a family of this size with income of £30 would get a family income supplement of £6 bringing household income up to £36. The eligibility levels are now increased every year (in July 1975 they went up by £6.50) and the supplement runs for a full 52 weeks irrespective of changes in circumstances.

Finally, there is the help in kind given to families with children. Families will obviously be affected, for example, by whether free school meals are provided for all children or only some, or by whether there is free milk or vitamins. Receipt of FIS does, for example, also entitle the family to free school meals, free milk, prescriptions and vitamins which in themselves may be worth £1 or more extra a week. In any comprehensive analysis of living standards such benefits would need to be taken into account.

It is thus clear that we have at present a wide range of different forms of benefit for children. For any particular family the value of each one, and the net value of all combined, vary for all sorts of reasons other than relevant differences such as variations in family needs. The aim for the future, as Barbara Castle argued, is for 'a single universal scheme of family support rather than the assortment of different and conflicting benefits' (*Hansard* 13 May 1975).

The Child Benefit Act

The Child Benefit Act, which as a Bill weaved its way through parliament during the first seven months of 1975, received its Royal Assent in August. It envisages three or more stages in the introduction of new child benefits. The first stage is the extension of family allowances to the first children of single-parent families in April 1976. The government intends to extend them to the first child of all other families a year later. Child tax allowances will be phased out gradually, and the scheme is not expected to be fully operational until 1979, when child benefits will be paid to all children and will take the place of the existing family allowances and child tax allowances. Even then, however, the child benefits will be at one rate for all children of all ages and only after 1979, if at all, will differential rates be introduced.

What will the child benefit scheme achieve? Stage one, the extension of family allowances to the first children of single-parent families, will help an officially estimated 255,000 families in 1976: 45,000 of these – the families with incomes below the tax threshold who are not on SB and not claiming FIS – will benefit by the full £1.50 a week. The 210,000 others, however, will not receive the full £1.50. This is first because the family allowance is taxable and the family will therefore have to pay tax on it if its income is above the tax threshold. Secondly, those who are receiving FIS will, because of this, have the value of the family allowance reduced by 75p. Those on SB will not benefit at all because monies received for family allowance will be deducted in full from the SB scale rates.

Stage two, the extension of family allowances in 1977 to the first child of two-parent families will mean that henceforth child benefit will be paid for every child in all families (rather than just the second and subsequent ones). This will extend payment to seven million extra families, three million of whom are single-child families and four million have two or more children. The total number of children receiving benefit will double. To the extent that child tax allowances are at the same time phased out and replaced by a tax-free cash payment, those families will gain most who, because they were not liable for tax, derived no benefit from tax allowances.

Because child tax allowances are paid to the father and the new tax-free cash payments will go to the mother, this changeover may also result in a redistribution of income within the family. The government welcomes this. Indeed in the debate on the 1972 Conservative Party Green Paper on the Tax Credit Scheme, Barbara Castle had presented a petition of over 300,000 signatures to parliament demanding that 'any support for children should be in the form not of a tax credit paid to the father but of a cash allowance payable to the mother through the post office' (*Hansard* 13 May 1975). The trade union movement also officially welcomes this formula. The Conservative Party, however, seems less enthusiastic. In the debate on the Second Reading, its spokesman, Norman Fowler, said that 'clearly there is a danger here that the reduction in take-home pay could – I put it no higher – trigger off a new round of wage demands'; he suggested showing the amounts paid to the mother on the father's pay slip. The importance of the distribution of income within the family has long been established (Young 1952). The National Consumer Council (1975), in some recent research into housekeeping allowances, found that wives and children were often losing out relative to their husbands. So Barbara Castle is right to stress this aspect of the new Act.

The final phase envisaged by the Act concerns the period after 1979. The Act provides for the possibility of paying the tax-free cash benefits not just at one rate for all children but at differing rates depending on the age of the child and other factors relevant for assessing variations in needs. There is no guarantee that this will happen. Nor is there any obvious reason why it cannot be done right from the start. I take up these and other criticisms later.

In general terms the Act has been welcomed from all sides. The Conservative spokesman in the debate on the Second Reading began with the words 'Let me say first that we welcome the Bill.' He went on to say that this was because, as Conservatives see it, 'the Government have (with the new Act) accepted part of the (Conservative) tax credit scheme. We sincerely hope that they will accept the rest.'

The Child Poverty Action Group also relate family endowment, as they call it, to a wider context, but stress that:

The fact that we have recommended a multiple strategy should not be allowed to obscure the central importance of family endowment. In Britain today there are ten million employed people with children . . . We believe it [family endowment] is perhaps the most important policy element of all the alternatives open to the Chancellor at the present time. For at whatever prospective level, a minimum wage cannot protect families from inflation and cannot ensure that families are lifted out of poverty. Family endowment is, in our view, the real kernel of the Social Contract (Field and Townsend 1975).

Nevertheless there have been many criticisms of detail and it is to these I now turn.

Criticisms of the new scheme

It is at present impossible to say what the level of benefits will be under the scheme. Its cost, the method of financing it and the rate of child benefit all remain to be decided. The fact that they are to be decided 'appropriately to the circumstances that obtain next year (1976)' (*Hansard* 13 May 1975) is worrying, given that 1976 is to be a year of big cutbacks in public expenditure and especially since 'the scheme is, of course, potentially expensive, and . . . will have to be settled in the light of the economic prospect of the time'.

Barbara Castle gave an illustration to show how the scheme will work. She assumed that the child tax allowance of £240 a year for children under 11 would be replaced by child benefits, and she worked out the amount that would thus be made available for each child. This was £1.94 a week. The poorer families below the tax threshold but not already on social security benefit would stand to gain the full £1.94 for the first child and 44p for each other child (they would previously already have been getting £1.50 family allowance). This version of the scheme would involve no cost to the Exchequer but it would mean that better off families would lose out. Every extra 1p added to this rate of £1.94 would involve a net cost to the Exchequer of about £6½ million a year net of saving on other social security benefits.

Michael Meacher asserted in the debate on an amendment to the Bill that 'there can be no question that families are to be singled out for extra taxation as a result of the Bill' (*Hansard* 7

July 1975). But if the so-called 'no cost' version of the scheme was implemented, this would mean in practice that other families with children were bearing the full cost of the extra monies paid to one-child families and those with incomes below the tax threshold. Earlier I showed families in general have been penalised relative to childless households and it is important therefore that the latter do in fact bear their full share of the costs of redistribution.

In the earlier part of this chapter I showed that child tax allowances had been allowed to decline substantially in value during the last 15 years. What guarantees are there that this will not happen with child benefits? With social security benefits now legally tied to rise in line with earnings and prices, the case for indexing this new benefit seems hard to resist, but Barbara Castle does not agree. She has argued that 'indexation of the child benefit is inappropriate. National insurance benefits are major means of support when earning capacity is interrupted, but the child benefit is a tax-free supplement to families whose major source of income is earnings. Clearly maintenance benefits must be capable of moving automatically in line with changes in the cost of living. The child benefit is in a different category' (*Hansard* 7 July 1975). This seems unconvincing. If the government promises help with the 'cost of a child', the real value of this form of support surely needs to be preserved just as much as, for example, widows' benefits which, not being subject to an earnings rule, are likewise paid in addition to any earnings.

As for more specific criticisms, a main one is that the benefits do not pay regard to differences in the needs of children of different ages. The CPAG provide detailed arguments why it should. Up to the present both supplementary benefit for children and child tax allowances have varied by age, as shown earlier. CPAG explain that there is now much evidence of the substantial needs of the older dependent child and argue this must be acknowledged in government policy.

The simplest thing to do in the immediate future, they say, would be to maintain three kinds of endowment for the age groups previously taken for child tax allowances. Pending the results of the recommended review of different rates by the Royal Commission on the Distribution of Income amd Wealth, they recommend the following rates be put into effect:

Age	Family endowment	
	as % of earnings	*Amount October 1974*
Under 11	6½	£3.20
11 – 15	8	£3.90
16 – 17	9½	£4.70
18 and over	11	£5.40

CPAG argue that, as part of 'a phased programme, over the next ten years', the government should 'increase the value of benefits in relation to average earnings. We propose a target . . . as follows: for those aged 11, 10% of average earnings; for those aged 11-15, 11½%; for those aged 16-17, 13% and for dependent children of 18, 14½%. On the assumption of average earnings of £62, this would mean that a couple with two children aged under 11 would receive £12.40 in child benefits' (Lister 1975). In addition CPAG argue that 'the presence of very young children often means loss to the household of one parent's earnings', and for tackling this they propose shifting resources from the married man's tax allowance to some form of home responsibility allowance.

Within any strategy to help families with children, it is important to recognise the special needs of one-parent families. Even with the new proposals, it does not look as if these needs will be adequately met. In October 1975, 15 months after the publication of the Finer Report, the ·House of Commons debated its recommendations for the first time. Barbara Castle took the opportunity to 'examine how far we[the government] have got, what remains to be done and the implications for public expenditure' (*Hansard* 20 October 1975).After reminding the House that 'it is 645,000 families and one million children we are talking about', and acknowledging that 'the case for some form of special help for one-parent families has been proved', she went on to say that 'a non-means-tested Guaranteed Maintenance Allowance would cost £400 million net of any savings on SB, FIS, etc' and that the government 'can only lift lone parents off SB altogether at a cost we simply cannot afford at the present time. I want to be honest with the House and tell the Members frankly that there is no early prospect of our being able to introduce a new special benefit for lone parents, certainly not one which would lift them off SB.'

So there is no bright future ahead for one-parent families. There have been improvements for some of them through the introduction of special tax allowances for lone parents and through lone fathers on SB no longer being required to register for work. Barbara Castle is, in addition, considering introducing a preferential earnings disregard for them in the future. But all this, even coupled with the extension of family allowances to the first child in one-parent families from April 1976, still leaves unsolved the bulk of the problem of income poverty in one-parent familes.

Conclusions

In this chapter I have been concerned with the incomes and needs of families, both in relation to childless households and as between families of different types or size. I have argued that families in general and certain families in particular ought to be in line for more help from the government. I then tried to critically examine how far the Labour government's new child benefits will meet these needs both in 1976 and in the longer term. A full assessment at the present time is impossible mainly because the 1975 Act dealt only with the benefit structure and left the financial details to be fixed at later dates. Until we know the levels of benefit and the method of financing them, we cannot judge how adequately the scheme will help in meeting family needs.

Nevertheless we already know that, whatever the levels, the cash payments will be as of right, ie not means tested) and ultimately tax free. This is certainly welcome. The fact that the benefits will all be at the same rate, and that they will not rise automatically year by year in line with average earnings or prices is however a cause for regret, as is the fact that there is inadequate provision for one-parent families.

I would like to end Part 1 by thanking Tony Atkinson, Frank Field, Adrian Sinfield and Peter Townsend for their help, although of course they may not agree with all I have said.

References

A.B. Atkinson (1975) 'Income Tax and Income Maintenance' *Journal of Social Policy* 1975 vol. 4 no. 1

F. Field and P. Townsend (1975) *A Social Contract for Familes* Poverty Pamphlet no. 19, Child Poverty Action Group

R. Lister (1975) *Social Security: The Case for Reform* Poverty Pamphlet no. 22, Child Poverty Action Group

Ministry of Social Security (1967) *Circumstances of Families*, HMSO

National Consumer Council (1975) *For Richer, For Poorer: Some Problems of Low-Income Consumers*

R. Titmuss (1962) *Income Distribution and Social Change*, Allen & Unwin

P. Townsend (1972) 'Foreword' to D. Bull (ed.) *Family Poverty*, Duckworth

M. Young (1952) 'Distribution of income within the family' *British Journal of Sociology* vol. III no. 4

2 Services

How far are people affected by changes in health and welfare services? Some recent developments may have helped particular kinds of deprived people. But the cuts in services seem bound to hit hard at those who most depend on them.

6   Gains and losses in health and welfare

PHYLLIS WILLMOTT

Until the end of 1973, although there were plenty of grounds for discontent, the climate in health and welfare services was – as it now seems – in general quite bright. There were certainly plenty of criticisms, for example about the quality of services, the inequalities of provision, the misuse of resources, the unmet needs of specific groups, the post-reform disillusion with Seebohm and the pre-reforms fears for health service reorganisation (Willmott 1974). But all these worries were raised in a context of a general belief and confidence in continuing progress – or at least expansion. A check on promises made as late as the autumn of 1973 shows that it included plans for more nursery school places; more hostels for young homeless people; more training facilities for social workers; more meals on wheels; more money for citizens advice bureaux; an increase in the numbers of disabled people benefiting from services and so on (Slack 1974).

A very different picture emerges from a look at developments following the crisis in December 1973 (which was followed by three months of the three-day week). In the spring of 1974 cuts were announced in both the health and personal social services, swiftly followed by the first of what later seemed like a rash of circulars containing ominous phrases like 'go slow' or 'abating growth' (Department of Health and Social Security 1974a, 1974b). By the autumn of 1975 the government were demanding nothing less than 'an overall standstill in expenditure for 1976-77', and warning of the unavoidability of 'further substantial economies' for 1977-78 and 1978-79 (Department of Health and Social Security 1975a).

Just how much things had changed had been made clear, in April 1975, in public statements by the Secretary of State responsible for local authority spending, and the Secretary of State responsible for the health and welfare services. The former, Anthony Crosland, speaking at the annual conference of the Association of District Councils, looked back on the increases of 8 to 10% in real terms that had taken place over the preceding three years and said, 'That rate of increase simply cannot go on. We are in a different world from the one we have been used to.' Three months later his message was cast in even harsher terms – there was to be no increase at all. Similarly, Barbara Castle, in a speech in July 1975 to the National Association of Health Authorities said:

> We have been used to a pretty steady annual growth, which has enabled us not only to cope with the extra demands arising from demographic factors, most notably the increase in the elderly population, and with the extra costs of new drugs and treatment, but also to make real progress in development. However, I think we shall be very lucky if in the next three or four years we see any real growth whatever in the National Health Service.

So much for the events which have over the past two years led to an almost complete reversal of expectations and hopes for health and social welfare services. The assumptions in 1972-73 were substantially those of continuing growth; those in 1976 are of substantial – some would say draconian – cuts. An important question for this chapter is what the likely effects of these will be, but over the last year or two various new policies have been implemented. However overshadowed they may now be, they must be reported and set in context.

Family planning
The Family Planning Association has rightly commented that 1974 was 'one of the most momentous years for family planning in this country since the birth control movement started this century' (Family Planning Association 1975). Modestly, the Association itself did not make much of its own large part in a campaign that forced governments against their will to change

tack, first from a policy of charging the economic cost for family planning supplies – except for certain specified groups – then to a normal prescription charge and finally to a comprehensive free service (Department of Health and Social Security 1974c). Thus a service which includes both free consultation and contraceptives, without restriction by age, residence or maritalstatus, and as part and parcel of the reorganised Nationa Health Service, began in April 1974. A disagreement between the government and general practitioners over fees held up full implementation of the servce. But since July 1975 any general practitioner can, and all health service clinics (or the Family Planning Association acting as agents) must offer a wholly free service.

Even though for some time to come the use of family planning facilities is likely to be in inverse relationship to poverty, the new scheme has undoubtedly improved the prospects of use by the poor. This is, first, because there is no 'deterrent' effect of payment and secondly, because through GPs and hospitals the service will become more accessible.

Prescription, dental and optical charges
There have been no changes in the levels of charges but there have been one or two minor amendments in favour of poorer people. First, in April 1974 (after an 18 months time lag) an adjustment was made to take into account the change in the compulsory school leaving age from 15 to 16 years: children up to 16 are now exempt from prescription charges. At the same time, women on reaching their retirement age of 60 became eligible for exemption (formerly they were not normally eligible until they reached 65).

In November 1974 there was a simplification in the means by which some people on low incomes could get help with dental or optical charges. Those who are on supplementary benefits, or getting family income supplement or free milk or vitamins (because of low income) and those exempt from other prescription charges on grounds of income, have now only to sign a form provided by the dentist or optician, instead of having to apply to local security offices.

Whether or not these changes will improve the take up of dental and optical services remains to be seen. It will, as always, depend on improving knowledge of their rights on the part of those eligible (which in turn must include improving the awareness of dentists and opticians and others who are in a position to inform those likely to be eligible).

Improving take up

Progress on the general problems of take up seems to have been negligible, although after much delay the Department of Health and Social Security (DHSS) has started some experiments to develop a multi-purpose benefit form. One, piloted in Liverpool, covered five benefits (including supplementary benefits and rent and rate rebates). Another, tried out in Shropshire, covers most local authority means tests, plus health service charges, but excludes supplementary benefit and family income supplement. The advantages hoped for from a multipurpose claim form are that it will save people supplying the same information over and over again and make it easier for them to obtain everything for which they are eligible. It is recognised, however, that an all-purpose form, which is inevitably longer and more complicated, may prove to be as unacceptable to those it is meant to help as the individual forms it is designed to replace. The most recent figures on take up – or more accurately non-take-up – remain as depressing as ever (*The Times* 14 October 1975).

Certainly with the present web of means tests there is an urgent need for further action – but what? As I argued in *Poverty Report 1974*, advertising to increase take up is both expensive and, as a one-off job, short term in its effects. For this reason the growing number of full-time welfare rights officers is encouraging. There are now close on 100, of whom about 20 are employed by local authorities. Another encouraging sign has been an apparent reluctance to introduce new means tests. But an anxiety about the future (as I suggest later) must be whether this direction can be maintained.

Progress and setbacks for the disabled

In 1973 the DHSS published, as it had promised, more detailed information on the kinds and amount of practical help for the disabled and elderly (additional to that from such well-established services as home helps or meals on wheels) which were supposedly more generously available following the Chronically Sick and Disabled Persons Act 1970. Some 143,000 households were helped in 1973 by installation of telephones, provision of television, radios, other personal aids, or by adaptations to their homes (Department of Health and Social Security 1973). During 1974 a further 200,000 households received help (Department of Health and Social Security 1974d). The numbers helped, for example, with telephone rental more than doubled (from 12,105 in 1973 to 28,800 in 1974) and there was a substantial increase (from 11,309 to 17,500) in those for whom minor adaptations to their homes were carried out. Most of this help, as with home helps and meals on wheels, went to elderly people. Although many of those were also disabled, some of the help given was to those simply suffering the 'normal' disabilities of old age.

There has been continuing increase in the number of those registered as disabled with local authorities, particularly to 'general classes' (that is, all those other than the deaf or partly deaf and the blind or partially sighted). Between 1970 and 1974 the numbers of this 'general class' of disabled people registered has more than doubled (from 234,100 to 497,200) and by 1975 had reached 580,000. However, research has shown it cannot be assumed that registration ensures receipt of all the help needed or indeed any help at all (Office of Population Censuses and Surveys 1971). In any case these increased numbers may now in part reflect the progress made by local authorities, not in giving help but in implementing section I of the Chronically Sick and Disabled Persons Act 'to inform themselves of the numbers and needs of handicapped people'. On the other hand, because registration is not a prerequisite for getting help from social services departments (although it is for getting additional help under the rent rebate scheme), there are known to be many disabled people who are unregistered but who are, as the DHSS ambiguously phrase it, 'in touch with local authority social service departments' (Department of Health and Social Security 1973).

To sum up, though increasing numbers of the elderly and disabled have been getting domiciliary help of various kinds, services are far from meeting known, let alone unknown demands even with this expansion. A recent report of the Family Fund suggests that for disabled children the picture is even blacker (Bradshaw 1975).

Apart from changes in social security (discussed in Chapter

4), another important issue for the disabled has been the battle of the 'trike'. After months of protest at the delay in publication, *The Report on the Mobility of Physically Disabled People* (Department of Health and Social Security 1974e), came out; it added strength to the flourishing campaign of a combination of pressure groups like DIG and the Disabled Drivers' Association, since it proposed replacing invalid tricycles with small cars. The Report's argument was partly based on the evidence that the tricycles were unstable and therefore less safe, but also that the most severely disabled of all – those unable to drive – could for the first time be helped: although unable to use a 'trike', they could use a car if they had someone to drive it for them. This would have substantially increased the costs, and the Report recommended that eligibility should be limited to those who needed a vehicle to get to work or full-time education or to maintain their families. It also recommended that there should be a means-tested mobility allowance for other disabled. Thus, while in some ways aiming to be fairer, the proposal would not have helped most of the *very* severely disabled, and would have made worse the position of some of the severely disabled by taking away from them their right to a 'trike'.

The government rejected the proposals. Instead it has introduced its own scheme for a 'mobility allowance'. This allowance is a non-contributory social security benefit of £260 per year, with eligibility based primarily on disability and not on income at all. The allowance is taxable, which means (although there will inevitably be anomalies) it will generally give rather more help to those in greatest financial need. Disabled drivers and disabled non-drivers (including severely disabled children) will benefit as the scheme gradually comes into force over the next three years, from January 1976. Those who wish to retain their 'trike' (and, despite the many criticisms of it, some do) will be able to. The Minister for the Disabled, Alfred Morris, writing about the scheme explained, 'The great advantage of giving money instead of hardware, is that people can spend it as they like' (*The Times* 26 September 1975). The fact that the scheme includes children marks progress from the early plans as described in last year's *Poverty Report*. It is of course arguable that the scheme does not go far enough; yet, despite continuing concern over the serious defects of the 'trike', it cannot be denied that it is in some ways a step forward. No one is worse off, and 100,000 severely disabled will be better off.

So long as the present allowance is accepted as a first step (and, more immediately, is at the very least not permitted to lose its value during this period of inflation and economic crisis), and so long as progress is made with the proposal to encourage favourable hire purchase arrangements for the disabled, there are grounds for cautious confidence in Barbara Castle's statement on the new arrangements that 'we are only at the beginning of this' (*The Times* 7 September 1975). It would be good to end on this hopeful note of progress for the disabled but one has to remember that, with rising unemployment, the disabled are amongst those worst hit. It is ironic that as it has become easier for some disabled to reach their work it has been, and will continue to be, harder for them to find a job.

The 'social wage'

One subject prominent in public debate in 1975, and explored by Chris Trinder in Chapter 4, is the so-called 'social wage'. In his Budget speech in February the Chancellor claimed that the value of this had increased by 12% in real terms since the previous year; he said that it had added an average of £15 a week to the 'effective real income' of every worker if the building of new houses, schools and hospitals were excluded, and about £19 if these were included. These calculations were made by adding up public expenditure on a wide range of services and working out the average per employed person per year. The figures from which Mr Healey's £15 a week are derived included government spending on pensions, subsidies, education and health, whereas his £19 included other services such as housing, libraries and museums, police and prisons, and the fire service.

The concept is obviously a useful one. The danger is that the notion of the average 'social wage' might be damaging rather than helpful to the poor, simply because it suggests that the not insignificant sum of £15 or £19 a week will be added to their income. In the end it is individual circumstances which decide which benefits will reach any particular family or individual. To take one instance, though average national figures might notionally be allocated to, say, families of child-bearing age for maternity services, they are in a practical sense irrelevant to the family of child-bearing age which has not had a birth during that year. Similarly, correcting the allocation of supplementary benefits to take account of the fact that the elderly or some lone parents are the biggest users of this service does not improve the financial position of those within these groups who nevertheless do not get it. Just as the 'average wage' figures for the manual worker conceal the affluence of some manual workers and the poverty of others, so too can the average 'social wage' lead to a distorted impression of state generosity which is at variance with individual experience, although entirely valid within the framework of its own rules and assumptions.

One way of coming to grips with the two sides of the truth, represented on the one hand by the 'average' and on the other by people as families, is to look at the specific experience of the latter. The first question is to assess – albeit only roughly – how the £15 or £19 per week 'social wage' in practice affects the lowest paid. The second is to illustrate how far the 'social wage', in combination with other changes over the past year or so in the health and welfare field, is likely to have improved their lot.

The following stories are taken from families interviewed in Lambeth, first in the winter of 1973 and again in 1974 or 1975. They were interviewed as part of the Lambeth Inner Area Study, which was one of three commissioned by the Department of the Environment and is discussed more fully in Chapter 10. The first interviews were carried out in a general survey in the area of study. The second interviews (with sub-samples of people from the first round) were aimed at finding out what use was made of certain social services by two types of household most likely to be in need of them – households with at least one person aged 70 or more and households with at least one child under 5, some but not all of whom were 'poor' in income, having not much above the supplementary benefit level (Department of Environment 1975a). Later research on multiple deprivation, discussed in Chapter 10 by Peter Willmott, revealed that a fifth of the households in these sub-samples were, in addition to being poor, among those with a large number of other 'deprivations' (Department of the Environment 1975b).

Thus these latter households are amongst the most deprived minority of those living in an inner-city area, and in addition

were at stages in life when they were most likely to need to call
on the kind of services which, in 'social wage' terms, are potentially most valuable. Their stories – of which three examples
are given below – serve to show how much the changes and
developments in services outlined in earlier paragraphs are
likely to materially improve their circumstances and perhaps,
to a more limited extent, to illustrate how the notion of the
average 'social wage' works out in individual terms.

In the winter of 1973, when first seen, Mrs A was living with
her two young daughters, aged four and two, in the attic floor of
a house where she had a kitchen, living room and bedroom. She
shared a bathroom with other tenants but had the sole use of a
toilet. She had no hot water and no garden. Her husband was in
prison and she was living on social security. Apart from social
security, she had benefited from use of the health service for her
children and a family planning clinic for herself. She had also
been helped by a 'welfare worker' to get pre-school play group
care, and occasional day nursery care for the children when she
visited her husband. The last time we saw Mrs A was in early
1975. By then her husband was out of prison and, with help
from a probation officer, had found work and was busy doing
up their flat. Things had improved for them but Mrs A said:

> To get things I like I'll have to go out to work. I'd like a
> washing machine but it's no good me working when I have to
> pay someone to look after the children.

Meanwhile she was still hoping:

> I give the gas and electricity money to Mum and Dad to look
> after until the bills come in. I also give them £2 savings. It's
> towards a washing machine or if anything comes up I've got
> it to fall back on.

While she was on social security Mrs A was probably close to
receiving the average amount in 'social wage', counting other
services she used at the time (and certainly, if one includes the
doubtful advantage to her of her husband's prison care, the
family was getting considerably above the average). During
this time she got other services like child welfare facilities (free
to everyone) and day care and family planning (free in her
circumstances). Now that her husband is home again – and she
is no longer a lone parent – she will have to pay for day care (so

far as she remains eligible for it) but, as a result of the 1974 changes, she will continue to get family planning services free. She has also, since April 1975, benefited from the increase in family allowance. On their low income she and her husband would possibly benefit from the easing of charges for dental and optical care, if they needed to. All the same, Mrs A does not feel very much better off now that her husband is working, but she blames this on inflation. As she sees it, the family's best chance for improvement will in a year's time, when her younger child starts school and she will be able to take a part-time job. The Lambeth survey suggests that her assumption is right. Among families with children aged under 16 the proportions in income poverty (as defined in Chapter 10) were as follows: wives working full-time, 0%; part-time, 6%; not working, 24% (Department of Environment forthcoming). The family would also be helped by rehousing, a more remote possibility.

Mr and Mrs B had been living for the past seven or eight months with their two daughters (one was a toddler and one a baby when we saw them in the winter of 1973) in an old block of council flats on the sixth floor. The Bs had arrived from Eire in 1972. For three months thereafter they were in bed and break-fast accommodation (found by social services) and living on social security. In the previous five years they had had six or seven moves. They have various complaints about their present flat – there is no lift, no garden and the bathroom is old-fashioned – but most of all they would prefer a ground floor flat. In addition to housing and social security, this family has over the past three years had a lot of help from the health service, including GPs, hospitals and child welfare services. By the second interview, in summer 1974, Mrs B had just reco-vered from a miscarriage, but her husband was not in good health. He had had a nervous breakdown arising from, he said, the stress caused by his wife's miscarriage plus the earlier housing and work worries. He was again unemployed.

This family, it seems reasonable to conclude, had benefited for the past three years from more than the average 'social wage'. Mr B was said to be 'extremely reticent about his employment prospects' and the interviewer felt he might be 'chronic unemployed' (he is in his early twenties). Since he is unskilled and lives in a district where there is little demand for such labour, the position of his family is unlikely to improve markedly whether he finds work or not (Department of the Environment 1974). Again, in theory, this family can benefit from the easier arrangements for dental and optical charges, and from free family planning, which (ignoring the possibility of religious objections), as a result of becoming more easily accessible, might be used with good effect from the long-term point of view.

Mr and Mrs C have lived for over twenty years on the ground floor of the terrace house in which they rent three rooms. They have no bath, and no hot water; they share the toilet with other tenants. When we first saw them in 1973 they were both 73 years old. Mrs C is very deaf and either does not have or does not use a deaf aid. Mr C, who before his retirement worked as a laundry hand in the health service, suffers badly from bronchitis in the winter. After his retirement Mr C took employment as a messenger and his wife worked part-time too. He did not seem to know about the earnings rule and, in trying to find out why his pension was so low, he formed a poor impression of 'social security' and has not been back since. He and his wife now live on their State pensions alone plus a small monthly occupational pension (£11 per month in 1973).

The Cs have obviously benefited over the past two years from the increases in pensions. The easing of the earnings rule has for them come too late. Both being old and disabled, they are undoubtedly eligible to benefit from the expansion of the domiciliary services discussed earlier. In fact they have so far not chosen to ask for any. Being retired as well as disabled, they do not benefit from the mobility allowance (although they can get free bus passes). The health services, of course, have been used a great deal by them. If various services to which they are entitled, such as rent and rate rebates, home helps, meals on wheels, and home adaptations and so on, were used and if their occupational pension were linked to inflation, their situation would be improved; and even more if radical improvements were made to their housing to provide them with suitable amenities. Actually, it must also be said that no one would be more amazed – if not indignant – than the Cs at the suggestion that they are the 'multiple-deprived'; as they see it, they are just 'hard up'.

What conclusions can be drawn from examples such as these? In the first place, no one would deny that the 'social

wage', especially that part of it which covers services like
education, health and social security in general helps everyone,
and in some cases the poorer more. What is more surprising is
how often, in spite of the 'social wage' and whether or not,
according to individual cases, more or less than the 'average'
reaches them, people and families who are deprived remain so.
It seems highly unlikely that this is only because poor people
fail to take up all the benefits for which they are eligible. On the
contrary, what is clear is how marginal in their effect on multi-
deprivation are many of the minor benefits for the poor. Free
school dinners, or a free pre-school playgroup place, or a home
help can no doubt ease the lot of the poor but in no way can they
fundamentally alter it. On the other hand, free family planning
(if it prevents an unwanted pregnancy), or effective health care
(if it prevents disability), or improved day care and after-school
services (if they enable a mother to work) can make a real
difference – can help to start them on the road out of poverty.
So too, of course, can other measures which materially increase
the family income, whether by some general tax credit system
or by higher family allowances or (for the disabled) mobility
allowances, attendance allowances and other 'compensating'
payments, or (for the elderly) the easing of earnings rules.

This underlines the importance of developing a far broader
framework of social policy than has been achieved so far. In the
search for a more effective approach to how the £25,000 million
of the 'social wage' is spent, one relevant event is the publication in 1975 of the report of the Central Policy Review Staff: *A
Joint Framework for Social Policies*. The key assumption in the
work programme proposed to the Cabinet is a joint and more
coherent approach to social policies, which will entail adjust-
ments in priorities, policies and administrative allocations by
the various departments and ministers concerned. It suggests
that the programme should in particular be 'concerned with
poverty in a wider sense: the condition of people whose com-
mand over resources generally – income, educational and
occupational skills, environment at home or at work, material
possessions – falls very seriously short of the average in the
community.' It has been argued that government interest in a
joint approach has 'as much to do with controlling public
expenditure as with coordinating and improving policy making' (*The Times Educational Supplement* 1975). But as long ago as

1967 Peter Townsend was asking for the creation of a Department of Social Planning 'which would be not so much a coordinating instrument as a long-term planning one' (Townsend 1975). In the present gloomy climate it is even more imperative that some kind of joint approach at central government level, and similarly at local level, should be developed.

Future outlook

The measures announced in August 1975 by Mr Crosland and confirmed in September with the publication of the circular (Department of Health and Social Security 1975a) promise 'an overall standstill in expenditure in 1976-77' which will inevitably lead to a reduction in the standard of local services, as will the cutbacks in expenditure in health services announced at the same time. The experience of the previous three years in trying to hold down growth in public spending has proved that it is in practice easier in these inflationary times to announce cutbacks than to ensure them. But the intention is clear; unlike the period from 1973 to 1975, the aim is no longer simply to slow down growth but to prevent it. Commenting on its proposals for savings and economies, the circular concludes: 'These measures will inevitably lead to a reduced capacity of the personal social services to meet demands made upon them by education, housing and health services and the courts.' The social welfare services are therefore in the unenviable position of being forced to face increased demands with decreased resources. It is not surprising that the first reactions to such a prospect were violent.

Directors of social services and local authority social services committees took the opportunity, in protesting against new cuts, to blame the government for earlier errors. A particular cause of dissatisfaction they picked out to re-emphasise was that of the impossibility of meeting all the new and extensive legislative responsibilities placed on them in recent years, that is even before the present situation arose. Devonshire County Council, for example, launched a campaign for the repeal of section 2 of the Chronically Sick and Disabled Persons Act which requires authorities to help the disabled get aids and services. It also wanted the new Children Act – which will impose additional obligations to do with the foster care and adoption of children – to be 'frozen'. This is also the view of the

Association of County Councils, whose social services committee estimates that they would cost £10 million to put into effect (*The Times* 28 October 1975). Professional associations such as the British Association of Social Workers, and voluntary organisations and pressure groups representing the interests of the mentally or physically disabled, the elderly, the single parent family and so on, have also voiced their alarm. Social workers, too, in various parts of the country, have demonstrated in protest about cutbacks which threaten to worsen already critical staff shortages and lead to lower levels of services (*Social Work Today* 1975a).

Where exactly the axe will fall, and in which direction, has been the main focus of concern. The circular purported to offer some guidance on this. It advised that domiciliary services (this would include home helps) should not be reduced, but that 'services that are provided generally, without regard to individual need, and on long term preventive activities' should be reduced. It is doubtful whether local authority social services committees will find this advice of much help. For one thing, few authorities have much scope for cutting back on the services that are provided 'without regard to individual need' because there are very few of them. For another – and leaving aside whether the home help service (which it is advised should not be cut back) is a 'long term preventive activity' (which it is advised could be) – the possibilities of choice in making cuts is severely limited. And just how difficult is the task faced by social welfare is made clear by the following examples.

Somerset expects to cut its budget by half a million over the next three years, probably on such services as home helps, meals on wheels and telephones and aids for the disabled (*Guardian* 22 October 1975). Gloucester plans to chip away £162,000 next year from disposable extras like transport serving old people's homes (*The Times* 29 October 1975). Kent, on the other hand, may well try to cut back mainly on residential care itself (which takes nearly half of the £16 million social services budget for the care of a minute percentage of the county's elderly) and so to find enough to pay both for cuts and for an increase in domiciliary services (*Community Care* 1975a).

For Wakefield district council, which has had in the past a steady increase in workload, there are plans to cut its budget by a quarter of a million pounds. Home helps will not be cut but recruitment of social work staff will be deferred. The Chairman of the social services committee commented, 'This will increase the risk to those already at risk – children and the elderly', but he also pointed out that 'holding back may damage society for two or three years – but the alternative is ever-increasing inflation until those services crumble altogether' (*Social Services* 27 September 1975).

In Coventry it is likely that home helps will not be replaced when they leave – and the result will be fewer clients served. Devon and Wakefield have no plans for any cutback in home helps, but know that as demand is still rising this will in practice mean a dilution of the service (Shearer 1975).

Another danger will be the temptation to increase charges, or introduce new means tests or reinforce old ones for services which, in the interests of those most in need, should not be rationed by income but only by medical or social criteria. Thus the National Council of Home Help Services has expressed fears that 'a slow-moving trend towards a totally free service following the abolition of minimum charges in many authorities' might well be reversed (*Community Care* 1975b). It seems too that the slow-moving trend towards at least standard minimum levels of welfare services in all areas might also be reversed.

Inevitably, and unfortunately, the effect of cuts in services interact on each other. The voluntary organisation Mind, for example, deplored the effect of a further capital expenditure cut (announced in August 1975) which will reduce the desperately needed increase in residential and day care places for the mentally handicapped. The result, predicts Mind, must be that patients in psychiatric or subnormality hospitals who no longer need medical care will have to remain there, even though 'in the long run, it is less expensive to keep people in the community rather than in hospitals' (*The Times* 12 August 1975). The sacrifice of 'long term preventive activities' (as the circular puts it) to short term expediency could be the most disastrous and unacceptable result of the crisis.

Conclusion

The purpose of this review has been to look at the effects on the poorest sections of society of recent changes in health and welfare services. A main theme (as in the chapter on the same subject in *Poverty Report 1974*) has been that it is too often the poorest who *in proportion to their need* benefit least from public services. The prospect is that in the current climate of economic stringency, myopic decisions may be made which will have the effect of pushing the balance even further against their interests. It is no doubt true that, after the rapid growth of recent years, some rethinking on policies would pay dividends, and even that the need for cuts might lead to some improvements in the allocation of current social welfare budgets. Certainly, along with strong protests at the cuts, this was one view presented at the 1975 annual conference of the British Association of Social Workers (*Social Work Today* 1975b). But any such gains that can be derived from *within* social welfare are not likely to provide dramatic results. Short of a miracle, five loaves and two fishes cannot be made to feed the multitude, however well they are shared out: and the fact remains that 'the most important feature in public expenditure on the personal social services is that a relatively short but rapid rate of growth has almost obscured the very low base line on which that growth has built' (Personal Social Services Council 1975).

This cannot be said of the health service, whose resources amount to more than six times as much social welfare's resources and which, with all its widely publicised deficiencies, offers in general far more of value to the poor, and also has far more scope for doing better within its present resources (Department of Health and Social Security 1975b).

However, the threat to both health and welfare is much the same. The temptation, for example, of cutting costs by increased charges or the introduction of new means tests, which would as usual be hardest on the poorest, must be resisted. The cost of the cuts must be made to fall on those who can most easily bear them. But this will mean looking not at the 'cost' just of health or just of social welfare – or, even more narrowly, of prescriptions or meals on wheels – but at the costs of all public services and their respective contributions in combating the fundamental deprivations of the poor.

References

J. Bradshaw (1975) *The Prevalence of Children with very Severe Disabilities in the UK*, Family Fund Research Project Paper

Central Policy Review Staff (1975) *A Joint Framework in Social Policies*, HMSO

Community Care (1975a) 5 November 1975

Community Care (1975b) 3 September 1975

Department of the Environment (1974) *Lambeth Inner Area Study: Labour Market Study* (IAS/LA/4)

Department of the Environment (1975a) *Lambeth Inner Area Study: Local Services: Consumers Sample* (IAS/LA/9).

Department of the Environment (1975b) *Lambeth Inner Area Study: Poverty and Multiple Deprivation* (IAS/LA/10)

Department of the Environment (forthcoming) *Lambeth Inner Area Study: Second Report on Multiple Deprivation*

Department of Health and Social Security (1973) *Annual Report*, HMSO

Department of Health and Social Security (1974a) *Local Authority Circular 11/74*, HMSO

Department of Health and Social Security (1974b) *Local Authority Circular (74) (36)*, HMSO

Department of Health and Social Security (1974c) *On the State of the Public Health, Annual Report of the Chief Medical Officer for 1973*, HMSO

Department of Health and Social Security (1974d) 43 Annual Report, HMSO

Department of Health and Social Security (1974e) *Report on the Mobility of Physically Disabled People*, HMSO

Department of Health and Social Security (1975a) *Local Authority Circular (75) (10)*, HMSO

Department of Health and Social Security (1975b) *First Interim Report of the Resource Allocation Working Party: Allocations to Regions in 1976/77*, DHSS

Family Planning Association (1975) *43rd Report and Accounts 1974-1975*

Office of Population Censuses and Surveys (1971) *Handicapped and Impaired in Great Britain*, part 1, HMSO

Personal Social Services Council (1975) *Data on the Personal Social Services: Report 1975*

A. Shearer (1975) 'Help at home', *New Society* 9 October 1975

K.M. Slack (1974) 'Social administration digest' *Journal of Social Policy*, vol 3, part 2, April 1974 Cambridge University Press

Social Work Today (1975a) BASW News, 13 November 1975, vol 6, no. 16 British Association of Social Workers

Social Work Today (1975b) Conference issue, 30 October 1975, vol 6, no. 15 British Association of Social Workers

The Times Educational Supplement (1975) 30 May 1975

P. Townsend (1975) 'The need for a social plan' *Sociology and Social Policy*, Allen Lane

Phyllis Willmott (1974) 'Health and welfare' in M. Young (ed.) *Poverty Report 1974* Temple Smith

Though there have recently been some hopeful advances in housing policy, action still falls far short of what is needed. On top of the detrimental effects of the cuts, official policy has lacked consistency and direction.

7   Contradictions in housing

CHRIS HOLMES

Poverty in housing takes two forms. First, the cost of paying for their housing can accentuate the poverty of people on low incomes. Secondly, the poor condition and shortage of housing itself constitutes a form of poverty for those who are unable to get a decent home, even though their money incomes may be relatively high. The difficulty in reviewing housing programmes and policies through 1974 and 1975 is that almost every intervention affected a wide range of people fairly indiscriminately, and also caused repercussions through other parts of the housing market.

For example, the Rent Act (1974) protected furnished tenants of absentee landlords against arbitrary eviction. This law benefited many poor families with young children and some low income single people or couples. In addition to gaining security, they have also been able to benefit from getting their rents registered and repairs carried out – rights previously made inoperable by the fear of eviction. However, the Act has also benefited quite a large number of fairly well-off households in furnished tenancies, predominantly young single people. And to some extent at least – though there is no reliable evidence on the scale – it has reduced the number of furnished lettings available and made access harder for those wanting such accommodation. Even if full data were available it would be a complicated task to assess all the gains and losses. Without it the task is still more hazardous.

Housing costs

The cost of housing has been held down remarkably effectively through the last two years. In the rented sector the major reason was the rent freeze introduced by the new Labour Government under the Counter-Inflation Act (1973) on 8 March 1974. This prevented any increases in rents in the public and private sector for 12 months, except where improvements were carried out. Subsequently, the Housing Rents and Subsidies Act (1975) restored to local authorities the freedom to fix rents for their own dwellings, replacing the machinery and criteria set up by the Housing Finance Act (1972). But it is estimated that council rents will rise on average by no more than 12% in the year ending 31 March 1976.

In the privately rented sector it is not possible to estimate the level of increases over 1975-76, but it seems probable that it will be significantly lower than the overall rate of inflation. The Housing Rents and Subsidies Act (1973) has stopped the phased de-control of the remaining controlled tenancies, and these can now be converted to regulated tenancies only where all basic amenities are provided and a qualification certificate obtained. The Rent Act (1974) brings protected furnished lettings under the jurisdiction of the Rent Officer, and means that the 'fair rents' that are set should exclude scarcity. Despite disquiet in some areas over the rents being fixed by rent officers, it is certain that many furnished tenants are now able safely to apply for rent reductions and get lower rents charged.

Housing prices have also been rising more slowly than prices generally over the last two years. Between June 1971 and June 1973 house prices rose on average by 79%. Over the same period average earnings rose by only 31%. As a result, thousands of prospective buyers, especially young couples, were priced out of the market. Until mid-1974 the building societies were suffering from an acute mortgage famine, eventually relieved by the loan of £500 million from the government to increase mortgage lending and encourage a revival of private house building. By 1975 money was flowing back steadily to the building societies and in April deposits reached a new record level, bringing the money available for lending up to £624 million. However, the government and building societies have been meeting regularly to review the interest rates and lending levels, and the societies have been allowing liquidity ratios to rise rather than risk excess demand in the still severely deflated private house-building market. Consequently, a renewal of the house price spiral has so far been avoided to date and prices have remained relatively stable, especially at the top end of the market.

In many ways the stability of housing costs is to be welcomed. The rent freeze, in particular, helped many poorer households. As Craven (1975) has shown, the public rented sector contains a very large proportion of the most vulnerable people. Taking the bottom three deciles of the income range, ie the bottom 30% in terms of household income, 41% were in public rented property in 1972, and this percentage has been increasing steadily over the 60s.

> Moreover, while household incomes are relatively low in the public sector, disposable per capita income may be even lower because the families tend to be larger: 37% of people in the public sector in 1971 were in households containing five or more persons; while the comparable figures for owner-occupiers, privately rented furnished accommodation and privately rented unfurnished accommodation were 25%, 17% and 21% respectively. Furthermore, the public sector contains a relatively large proportion of single-parent families (Craven 1975).

In theory, of course, the poorest tenants could all be assisted by rent rebates and allowances. But the latest data on takeup rates shows that only 65% of council tenants eligible are receiving allowances, 25% of private unfurnished tenants and 10% of private furnished tenants. In *Poverty Report 1974* Willmott welcomed the newly introduced rebates and allowances as an important step towards reducing the housing costs of the poor, but stressed the problem of take up which was already apparent. Experience since confirms the failure of means-tested benefits to reach those eligible adequately, especially in the privately rented sector. Despite its indiscriminate character the rent freeze was an income progressive measure which ensured that all poor tenants enjoyed the benefits.

None the less, policies which restrict increases in housing costs are likely to cause difficult problems in some areas. The stability of house prices has re-opened access to house purchase to more households on average or just below average incomes, but it has also discouraged private builders from embarking on new schemes. The rent freeze was one more restriction on private landlords, making it even less likely that repairs would be carried out, improvements made or future lettings given once the present tenants leave. And in the public sector the rapidly escalating deficits on housing revenue accounts contributed to by rent policies have increased the share of public housing expenditure consumed by subsidies rather than allocated to investment in new house building or improvement work.

To sum up, the poor have benefited in the last two years from the policies which have prevented housing costs rising nearly as rapidly as the rate of inflation. The restrictions on rent increases, both public and private, have been the most important measures. But the indiscriminate character of the policies has also caused adverse effects, particularly in relation to the quantity and quality of housing provided. This problem will be taken up again later in the chapter.

Social ownership and improvement

In January 1974 the former Conservative Government introduced the Housing and Planning Bill, whose main proposals had been foreshadowed in the White Paper *Better Homes: the Next Priorities* (1973). The Labour Opposition in Parliament critised the Bill vigorously during the Second Reading debate in Parliament, but none the less re-introduced an only slightly amended Bill following the February General Election. It was eventually enacted in July as the Housing Act (1974).

The new Act has two main purposes. First, it creates an entirely new subsidy system for registered housing associations, designed to encourage the rapid expansion of the most reputable and efficient of them. It does this by strengthening the powers and increasing the funds of the Housing Corporation, so that it can run the scheme for registering approved associations and provide finance for new schemes. And through the new Housing Association Grant all registered associations can get payments for approved housing projects from the Department of the Environment to meet the whole deficit between the market cost and the income from 'fair rents'. This is an extremely important innovation because it enables housing associations for the first time to be financially viable without having to depend either on charitable funds or on rate contributions. Since a high proportion of housing association work, especially in rehabilitation, is concentrated in poor areas, this represents a valuable injection of central government resources ·to inner urban neighbourhoods.

It is estimated that £212 million will be spent by the government in grants to housing associations in 1975-6. Comparable data are not available for previous years, but this expenditure undoubtedly represents a sizeable increase. In 1974 housing associations in England and Wales completed the building of 9,440 new homes and 5,295 were provided by acquisition and improvement. For the financial year ending 31 March 1976 it is estimated that approvals will be given for the provision of approximately 28,000 new homes and 13,000 by modernisation.

Secondly, the Housing Act empowers local authorities to create Housing Action Areas in the worst neighbourhoods of severe housing stress. This innovation was linked to measures for ending the higher grants being paid in intermediate and development areas since 1971, and to policies for curbing the abuse of the improvement grant system by property speculators. Briefly, local councils have new powers in Housing Action Areas (HAAs) for compelling owners to make improvements, for serving compulsory purchase orders and to be notified of any sales of tenanted property or evictions. In addition, owners are eligible for 75% grants – increased to 90% in cases of hardship.

The Act was significant in. its overt aim of concentrating resources, especially for the improvement of older housing, in the areas of greatest need. The criticism of the Act focused on the dangers of restricting activity in small geographical areas: this would be inappropriate where poor housing is spread in fragments across wide districts, and wholly ineffectual unless a large number of HAAs were declared quickly. It was also argued strongly that the proposed compulsory improvement procedures were likely to be slow, cumbersome and ineffectual. The spearhead of an effective strategy in stress areas needed to be the rapid and widespread use of compulsory purchase powers, so as to replace the mainly small and inefficient private landlords who have shown themselves unable or unwilling to make improvements for their present tenants.

The Labour Government's initial statements and actions suggested that such a broad interventionist policy would prevail. Circular 70/74 *Local Authority Housing Programmes*, issued on 19 April 1974, set out the plans for encouraging social ownership of rented housing in the worst areas of housing stress. In particular, local authorities were encouraged to buy up tenanted property where tenants were living in bad conditions or facing the threat of eviction. Priority was also given to the acquisition of empty property. Housing ministers emphasised repeatedly that the Housing Action Area powers were only one strand in the plans for encouraging the improvement of older property, and the first stage in an urban renewal strategy.

It is now possible to make at least a preliminary assessment of the new policies. First, the termination of the higher grants in development areas has undoubtedly led to a sharp fall in the take up of improvement grants. The rate of grant approvals dropped from the record level of 361,900 in 1973 to 231,900 in 1974 and only 99,300 in the first nine months of 1975. Broadly, improvement activity is now cut to nearly a third of its level only two years ago. It is now running at the same rate as 1970, before the major shift of housing policy towards rehabilitation began to take effect.

It is certain that the grant restrictions have stopped abuses of the system. Convincing evidence has been produced in recent years to show that, although the higher grants in poorer areas boosted demand and created desirable employment, those who benefited were often relatively well-off private owners or tenants on inter-war council estates already in reasonably good condition. They were not concentrated at all on the tenanted properties in the worst condition. In addition, grants were being abused in potentially attractive neighbourhoods, especially of inner London, to speed up 'gentrification' and aggravate the shortage of cheaper rented accommodation.

The fall in improvement work has, of course, been caused partly by the economic recession and restrictions on council spending. The ratio between private and public improvement is still just over 2:1, but both sectors contained some relatively low priority schemes. It is difficult to be sure at this stage, but it is probable that the collapse of improvement has adversely affected many people in poor living conditions.

Secondly, the policies outlined in Circular 70/74 led to a sharp increase in the scale of acquisition of tenanted houses by local councils. In 1974-75 £180 million was spent on buying up 23,000 properties. A high proportion of this was spent by inner London boroughs, but a large number of authorities were embarking on municipalisation programmes. It seems that the rate of purchase was speeding up considerably by the early months of 1975. Linked with the growing activity of housing associations, this represented a new and radical form of intervention into the privately rented sector, where the worst housing conditions are to be found.

But on 9 June 1975 a new Circular 64/75 *Housing Expenditure Changes* ended this policy. Apart from exceptional circumstances, local authorities were now given permission to buy only property that had been empty for at least six months or tenanted houses in housing action areas, priority neighbourhoods or general improvement areas. It is still planned that municipalisation spending in 1975-76 will be approximately £180 million, the same level as 1974-75, but this means a significant reduction from the rate of purchase reached by early 1975. The new circular marked the end of the broad interventionist policy across wide areas of housing stress advocated by the present government, and many housing experts, in discussions on the Housing Act (1974).

Still more seriously, the rate of Housing Action Area declarations has been slow, and activity within them limited. By 30 September 1975 63 HAAs had been declared in England and Wales. This must be set against estimates such as the assessment by a joint working party of officers from the Greater London Council and the London Boroughs Association that 150-200 Housing Action Areas are needed in London alone. To some extent the small number of declarations is merely a reflection of delays by local authorities in determining policy, and more HAAs are likely to be declared in the coming months. But the HAA approach cannot be seen as a major assault on the housing problems of stress areas.

A crucial factor in the weakness of the policy is the guidance given to local authorities on the powers to be used within HAAs. Circular 14/75, issued on 28 January 1975, discourages forceful action to replace private landlords, even though virtually all available evidence pin-points their reluctance or inability to carry out socially necessary improvements as the root cause of poor conditions.

The circular states that 'in general, proposals for large scale compulsory purchase orders soon after declarations will not represent an efficient use of resources and may in fact prejudice living conditions'. It takes a very cautious attitude to acquisition and a reliance on voluntary agreement for improvement, wherever possible. The result is that, even in the HAAs declared, the scale of improvement being carried out appears to be extremely limited. For instance, at the end of October 1975 the HAA declared by the GLC in the Birnam Road area of North Islington in February (the fourth in the country) had not resulted in any houses yet actually being bought (although negotiations were in progress for a number) with only four applications for improvement grants by private owners. On the evidence available, it seems extremely improbable that the planned level of municipalisation will be sustained, unless more HAAs are declared quickly or the criteria for purchase widened again. It would be impossible for 23,000 houses to be bought annually in the tightly restrictive categories now in force.

The least foreseen result of the Housing Act was the effect of section 105, which empowers the Secretary of State to limit expenditure by local authorities on improvement work. In the parliamentary debates on the Housing Bill, government ministers categorically denied that this clause would be used to restrict acquisition and improvement of privately rented property. Its only purpose was to curb reckless expenditure and channel resources to the areas of greatest need.

But in March 1975 local authorities were told by the government that their bids for money for improvement in 1975-76 had been cut from the £572 million requested to only £271.5 million. Despite the government's denials, it was refusing money not merely for inter-war estates and to curb overbidding, but as a direct limit on the resources for carrying out improvements on sub-standard older homes bought from the private sector.

The cuts had been foreshadowed in the public expenditure estimates published by the government in January 1975. These showed a planned reduction in local authority improvement spending from £422.7 million in 1974-75 to £296.7 million in

1975-76. Even more depressingly, expenditure for 1977-78 was forecast to total only £235 million.

As a result of fierce pressure, the government added an extra £44 million to the budget for 1975-6 and have been able to restore funds for the most damaging cuts in improvement programmes. A study group has been set up between representatives of local authority associations and the government to determine needs, priorities and programmes for future years. This should prevent the dislocation and bewilderment caused by the sudden exercise of section 105 powers in 1975, but it is still likely to remain as an unpopular and restrictive limit on council improvement.

Overall, the plans for redirecting improvement resources through the measures in the Housing Act have resulted in disappointment. The voluntary housing movement has been enabled to expand vigorously, and a greater share of improvement work is benefiting people in the worst housing conditions in stress areas. But the rate of rehabilitation activity has been cut severely, and this inevitably harms many people in sub-standard homes. The major programme of social ownership and improvement promised by the Labour Government in its early days is not now being realised. Improvement is being restricted to a relatively small number of rigidly defined geographical areas, and even within those the powers used are slow and cumbersome. The strategy fails to match in powers or resources the needs of poorly housed residents in stress areas.

New building

In 1974 the level of new house building sank to its lowest ebb for over 20 years. In total only 268,300 homes were completed. This should be contrasted with the record of 413,700 homes completed in 1968, and the target of the government White Paper *The Housing Programme 1965 to 1970* (1965) which stated:

> The rate of building will be pushed up as fast as resources and improving techniques allow. The first objective is to reach half a million houses a year by 1970. Even that, however, will not be enough . . . The 1970s should see still bigger programmes

To some extent that assessment would need revision in the light of the shift away from massive redevelopment towards policies of gradual improvement and renewal. But, despite such changes in policy, it is undeniable that the rate of house building has fallen to an unacceptably low level. The most recent assessment of overall housing need was made by the National Economic Development Office in 1972. Their conclusion was that 393,500 houses a year were needed in Great Britain for each of the years between 1972 and 1977. In practice, 319,100 houses were built in 1972, 293,600 in 1973 and 268,300 in 1974. That already leaves a shortfall of 300,000 houses over only three years.

Nevertheless, some modest improvements have been made during the past two years. In early 1974 the new Labour Government gave strong encouragement to local authorities to increase their house-building programmes. The cost yardstick was revised significantly. In the Budget the Chancellor of the Exchequer allocated an extra £350 million to housing programmes, especially for new building and the acquisition of privately built unsold houses. In addition, the government made a short-term loan of £500 million to the building societies to alleviate the severe mortgage famine. This was designed not only to assist house buyers immediately, but also to restore confidence in the building industry.

The results have been that public house building had risen from a seasonally adjusted level of 11,900 housing starts monthly in the first quarter of 1974 to 14,800 in the third quarter of 1975, and private house building had risen from, 11,400 in the first quarter of 1974 to 12,500 in the third quarter of 1975. In summary, this means that the level of starts had risen from a rate adequate for only 270,000 completions annually to almost 330,000. Against the background of the economic recession, this is an important and praiseworthy achievement.

Allocation and access

To what extent, however, will this increase result in better housing opportunities for the poor? How effectively do the policies and procedures for access to housing operate to relieve acute housing need? Unfortunately, the extent of reliable research into these questions is very limited, so that conclusive answers cannot be given. But some provisional answers can be given, and it is important to pinpoint certain significant developments in the recent past.

Very few new private houses go directly to people previously poorly housed. However, advocates of the 'filtering' argument claim that the sale of every new house, even if it is an expensive property, triggers off a long chain of sales and movements that ultimately benefits those in severe housing need. In practice, the process works less beneficially: the acceleration of household fission, ie the formation of new households, has meant that many new homes go to people previously well housed setting up their own home without releasing any extra accommodation. A Department of the Environment survey in 1973 found that 50% of new house sales did not involve the sale of any previous home.

Two developments in the mortgage market in recent months make this a serious issue. First the government decision to lift the ceiling on mortgages (except for a small quota) from £13,000 to £20,000 may make it easier for sellers of expensive homes to find a purchaser, but is unlikely to help poorer families even indirectly and will inevitably reduce the volume of funds available for mortgages on cheaper property.

Secondly, local authority mortgages for 1975-76 were halved by the government in the June 1975 Circular 64/75 *Housing Expenditure Changes*. In 1974 council mortgages totalled £455 million, representing 12% of all lending. The Labour Government had actively encouraged council lending on recovering office, and by the first quarter of 1975 council mortgage advances amounted to £184 million, 15% of the market. This was at an annual rate of over £700 million.

But in June 1975 the government decided to allocate an extra £100 million to the municipalisation programme and to local authority improvement – in response to the bitter criticism of the section 105 cuts – and withdrew the funds from the council mortgage budget. Moreover, the original government estimates had allocated only £350 million for this programme in 1975-76. The result was that local authorities suddenly received instructions to reduce mortgage loans to a level half that of 1974-75 and a third of that reached in the early part of 1975.

Traditionally, council mortgages have gone to applicants turned down by building societies. They have almost all been given to first-time buyers, predominantly on cheaper and older property. Firm evidence is not available, but it is almost certain that by early 1975 the overlap between building societies and local authorities had grown considerably. Some councils were becoming too indiscriminate in their lending policies.

But the abruptly imposed cuts meant that most authorities had to suspend their schemes almost immediately. The revised budget had already been allocated within the first few months of 1974-75. This made it impossible for any sensitive criteria for allocating mortgages to be applied, so that those who have suffered most are the poorer applicants who cannot satisfy the building society criteria for deposits, stable incomes and secure jobs.

Under pressure from the government, the building societies have agreed to release an extra £100 million to assist applicants who cannot obtain building society mortgages. This is a useful advance, but, since the societies have insisted that their normal lending criteria will still apply, it is unlikely to benefit the families who could only qualify for council mortgages. Unless the building societies are prepared to grant more 100% mortgages, to relax their income requirements and lend much more on cheaper pre-1919 property, the new arrangements will not help the applicants in greatest need.

Council allocation policies on homes to rent are also too often arbitrary and discriminatory. In 1969 the Cullingworth Report *Council Housing: Purposes, Procedures and Priorities* recommended radical changes in allocation procedures, but no firm government action has been taken to ensure implementation of those proposals, and very few reforms have been made. Many local authorities still impose a rigid qualification of several years' residence before any family can even be considered for rehousing.

Some authorities still use a 'date-order' system for allocation, based solely on the length of time on the waiting list, regardless of need. It is not unknown for council homes to be given out on the nomination of ward councillors. In a few authorities recently a ballot has been introduced for allocating homes to young couples not eligible for rehousing by the normal criteria – an innovation only too likely to reinforce the cynical view that the whole system is a lottery.

Perhaps the most serious failure towards the poor over the last two years has been the government's vacillations over the responsibility for homelessness. In February 1974 the Conservative Government issued a Circular 18/74 *Homelessness,* which set out the measures local authorities ought to adopt to help the homeless. It recommended that the responsibility for homelessness should be transferred from social service departments to the housing departments of the new district councils, and outlined a range of progressive policies for the discharge of those responsiblities.

Yet by the middle of 1975 about 100 housing authorities, almost a third of the district councils in England and Wales, had still not taken over responsibility. And the recommendations in the circular were still being widely ignored. Large numbers of authorities will not even accept responsibility for the priority groups defined in the circular (ie families with young children. one-parent families, elderly people and others with particular disabilities), let alone for all homeless people. Single people therefore are almost universally excluded from consideration. The threat of taking children into care is still used in some areas to deter homeless families from applying for accommodation; at the last count 2,777 children were in care in England and Wales for the sole reason that their families had no home. Some authorities refuse to accept responsibility for pregnant women, even at an advanced stage of pregnancy. Families are still split up. Extensive use is still being made of extremely costly and unsatisfactory bed and breakfast accommodation.

At the root of this chaos is the government's failure to impose a clear, legal obligation on housing authorities, with effective default powers. The 1972 Local Government Act amended the duty that had existed in the 1948 National Assistance Act to a purely discretionary power. This was met with a universal outcry from the organisations involved on a day-to-day basis with homeless people, and Sir Keith Joseph, then Secretary of State for Social Services, issued a directive in February 1974 reimposing the duty on social service authorities. This leaves the peculiar situation whereby housing authorities are expected to undertake a responsibility for homeless people, but have no obligation to do so, while social service authorities, who have been asked to transfer the responsibility, have a residual duty imposed by the directive!

In June 1974 the government promised to set up a wide-ranging review, but the Consultation Document was not published until May 1975. This document itself, whilst recognising that the current situation was unsatisfactory, stated that 'the government does not consider the present to be an appropriate time to introduce legislation'. However, on 19 November 1975, Anthony Crosland, Secretary of State for the Environment, announced an important change in government policy in his speech to the Joint Conference of Local Authority Associations in Eastbourne. It was clear that the review had revealed a widespread avoidance of responsibilities by the local authorities and had forced a major concession to the pressure for new legislation:

> I am disturbed to find that three-quarters of all housing authorities in England appear to take a rather limited view of their responsibilities . . . As a result I am clear that we must have a firm definition of where the responsibility lies. I therefore intend . . . to place a statutory responsibility for accommodation for the homeless upon housing authorities. Moreover, I intend that they shall have not only duties, but the powers that are – or may prove to be – needed to carry out their responsibilities.

It will be essential that the legislation does compel even the most intransigent local councils to provide accommodation, whatever the reasons for homelessness. And a timetable for a new law still has to be announced. But the statement does represent an important and desperately needed change in policy.

The conflict of objectives

The record of housing achievement during 1974 and 1975 is complex and confused, especially in relation to the alleviation of poverty. House building rates improved, improvement policy was concentrated more in the worst stress areas, housing costs have been held relatively stable. But acute inequalities persist, and recent public spending cuts have harmed the poor and badly housed most severely.

One significant change was the increase in public expenditure on housing from £2,739 million in 1973-74 to £3,615 million in 1975-76 – at constant prices. Public spending was increased by 25% in real terms, despite the severest economic problems. This represented a rise in housing's share of public expenditure from 6.4% to 9.4%.

Paradoxically, this increase has not been reflected in more new homes being built and older homes improved. Total capital expenditure on housing investment has remained constant over recent years. The major cause has been the rise in subsidies, particularly for council housing. The cost of subsidies has risen from £735 million in 1973-74 to £1,077 million in 1974-75 and an estimated £1,204 million in 1975-76.

The reason for this, however, is not the failure of rents to keep pace with the rate of price rises generally; indeed, council rents have been increasing more rapidly than inflation in recent years, except during the rent freeze. The explanation lies primarily in the effects of inflation in higher interest rates and escalating debt repayments. Debt charges on council housing increased by £300 million between 1973-74 and 1974-75 and it is estimated they will rise by £244 million in 1975-76, to a total of £1,270 million. Yet, as Webster (1975) has demonstrated, this increase is primarily due to a shift in the pattern of repayments, increasing the debt in the early years but ultimately reducing the real cost of council housing. None the less, its short-term impact on public housing deficits has been severe.

The Department of the Environment is now engaged in a wide-ranging review of housing finance, instigated by the Secretary of State, Anthony Crosland. It is expected that this will be completed in the first half of 1976 and will be followed by legislation. A key issue in this review is the conflict between housing investment and housing subsidies.

It is widely argued that a disproportionate share of public expenditure is now being consumed by policies for holding down costs at the expense of programmes for renewing and enlarging the housing stock. At its crudest the argument is expressed in terms of putting up council rents sharply or else not being able to afford to assist people in severe housing need. Implicitly, it reflects the tension between the objectives of *income maintenance* and the goals of *housing* policy itself.

A strategy against poverty

Expressed in those categories, the debate is barren. It will become deadlocked between the social forces seeking to preserve the living standards of working-class people and the pressures to make a stronger attack on the vast shortage of decent homes. It can only be resolved by a redefinition of the issue. What is lacking is a strategy against poverty.

The absence of such a strategy extends across the whole field of social policy, and could only be met by a comprehensive approach across the boundaries of separate government departments. But it is possible to outline its key elements in the sphere of housing costs and provision.

First, resources must be allocated as a high priority towards the areas of housing stress. The analysis of improvement programmes showed the inadequacy of current policies: the restrictions on municipalisation and local authority improvement, the limited powers and puny scale of Housing Action Areas. The acute concentration of disadvantage in housing stress areas has been documented by innumerable studies, yet government policies have consistently failed to channel a major share of house-building and rehabilitation activity to meet the needs of residents in those areas.

In addition, poor conditions and housing shortages persist in almost every area of the country. The intensity of multiple deprivation is less than in the stress areas, yet for those trapped in unsatisfactory conditions the need is still urgent. Area-based programmes must not, therefore, be a substitute for comprehensive efforts to relieve housing need wherever it is found.

In practical terms, the strategy requires increasing and sustaining a large house-building programme, particularly of rented homes. Local authorities and housing associations must be enabled to acquire sub-standard or empty properties, especially in stress areas, and investment in housing improvement must be greatly increased, particularly by lifting the ceiling of section 105 expenditure. And urgent consideration should be given to drastic powers enabling councils to take over control of vacant and poorly managed privately rented property without incurring immediately the major costs of acquisition.

Secondly, the housing costs of poorer households must be restrained. Rent rebates and allowances are one means for achieving this, but inadequate take up mars their effectiveness. Unless it is possible to devise a form of housing allowances which is financially practicable and extends as much help to the poorest income groups as does the present system of rent rebates and rent allowances, policies for limiting rent increases will continue to be necessary. The review of the rent freeze has

shown that it was successful in limiting costs for a group
significantly poorer, on average, than the community as a
whole.

The most regressive and least justified subsidies are to the
private sector. The system of tax relief for owner-occupiers cost
£755 million in 1974-75. Whilst assistance to first-time buyers
on lower incomes is essential, the bulk of tax relief benefits
better-off owners. Indeed, the rate of relief rises directly with
the level of income and the value of the house. At the very least,
reforms are needed which limit relief to the standard rate of
income tax, reduce the maximum limit from the present
£25,000, and restrict the period over which relief is granted.

It is also intolerable that local authorities should need to lend
money for mortgages from scarce public expenditure funds
when the building societies are flush with money. Some form of
social control of building society lending is essential to ensure
that a larger share of mortgages are used to help poorer first-
time buyers, especially through more 95% or 100% loans and
more advances on cheaper, pre-1919 houses.

In sum, what is needed is a consciously redistributive
strategy that directs resources towards helping the poor and
badly housed. The past two years have witnessed several radical and hopeful advances in housing policy, but the record has
been marred by the lack of decisive social objectives.

References

Better Homes: the Next Priorities (1973) Cmnd 5339, HMSO

Council Housing: Purposes, Procedures and Priorities (1969) Report of the Central
   Housing Advisory Committee of the Ministry of Housing and Local
   Government, HMSO

E. Craven (1975) *Social Priorities and Inflation,* Centre for Studies in Social
   Policy

Department of the Environment (1974), *Homelessness, Circular 18/74,* HMSO

Department of the Environment (1975), *Housing Expenditure Changes, Circular
   64/75,* HMSO

HousingProgramme 1965 to 1970 (1965) Cmnd 2838, HMSO

Department of the Environment (1974) *Local Authority Housing Programmes,
   Circular 70/74,* HMSO

P. Willmott (1974) 'Housing' in M. Young (ed.) *Poverty Report 1974,* Temple
   Smith

D. Webster (1975) 'Council house costs: why we should all calm down', *Roof,*
   October 1975, Shelter

In education as in other services there have been some gains. But the cuts are already biting and the big anxiety is about the future. The primary task is to ensure that the interests of the disadvantaged are protected.

8 Education on the defensive

STELLA DUNCAN and MICHAEL YOUNG

Two years ago the last *Poverty Report* to deal with education said that 'if the palm for 1973 is awarded to any Departmental Minister then from the particular point of view of this Report it should go to Mrs Thatcher'. Nursery education had received in that year more of a boost from her than ever before from any of her predecessors – ever means ever and any, any – and with a bias in favour of the most deprived districts. Educational Priority Areas (EPA) were still much to the fore. A little more had been done for handicapped children. The school-leaving age had been raised. Massive replacement of old primary schools had been announced.

Before the year was out much of the programme was undermined by the Barber cuts. In the following March the government fell. Mrs Thatcher was succeeded by Mr Prentice, a Secretary of State who was acutely aware of inequalities in the share out and take up of educational benefits. But he had the will without the means. Educational benefits have been two years on the retreat. In this chapter we look at what has happened in the period, concentrating on where the gap between rich and poor in educational terms is widest or where a narrowing could bring most help to those who are worst off.

Pre-school education
Against this background it was a matter for some congratulation that the Labour government continued to protect the £34 million assigned to nurseries in 1974-76. More than that, an

additional £4.3 million was offered to authorities to make good
places lost in the 1974-75 programme as a result of rising costs.
But inflation has cut further the places which can be provided
nationally from the 1975-76 allocations, though they are rather
more heavily loaded than in the previous year in favour of inner
urban areas.

Locally, it was difficult to find out what this meant in terms of
action. Money centrally assigned for nurseries was, as normal
with capital expenditure, not a grant but a permit to raise a
loan. Local authorities have to meet loan charges and on top of
that running costs once the nurseries open. On this account
about 20 authorities were reported to have turned down or
reduced their allocation for 1974-75 and a larger number, still
growing, are doing the same for the overlapping allocation for
1975-76. For this reason and also because of the prospect of
empty spaces in primary schools as numbers fall, it is difficult to
fault the approximate halving of funds for nursery classes
announced for 1976-77. Capital not taken up, and the additional £4 million, had been offered to authorities which made a
bid on grounds of social need. Lack of time must be making for
rough judgements – if indeed all the money can be used. Broadly, the counties have cancelled or cut their programmes while
the metropolitan authorities have gone ahead with theirs. The
effect has therefore been to benefit the needy areas. But there
are certainly many exceptions: country children deprived of
stimulus and contact with other children; areas poor for gener-
ations and unambitious; impoverished districts incorporated in
new authorities under pressure from ratepayers.

The new nursery units are just beginning to open. Will the
most deprived children find their way to them? When the
Department of Education and Science (DES) spelled out in
detail how nursery expansion could best take effect, they asked
authorities to consult with 'social service departments and
voluntary bodies' to give priority to the disadvantaged. Yet the
latest available information suggests that effective coordinating committees of those concerned with the under fives
have been set up only in a small minority of places, despite the
obvious problems when day nurseries, crèches and playgroups
come under the care of the social services and nursery classes
and schools under the education authority. No further lead has
come from the centre. A joint circular from the Department of

Health and Social Security (DHSS) and the DES advising cooperation has been in gestation for months.

Fortunately 1974-76 has seen some informal moves towards coordination – seminars and conferences – by those concerned with the under fives. In the field, an increase in the handful of nursery centres, combined day nursery and nursery classes, awaits the outcome of an evaluation by the National Children's Bureau. A few authorities, notably the Inner London Education Authority (ILEA), in collaboration with the social services departments of the London boroughs and with voluntary bodies, are experimenting with various combinations of child care and education, normally so incongruously separated. Classes attached to nearby primary schools are being built on day nursery sites; nursery nurses from day nurseries and child minders are going with children to nearby classes; social service departments are being asked to provide care end-on for children from some schools and nursery classes (Inner London Education Authority 1975). These and other combinations of day nurseries and day fostering with nursery classes and playgroups were the forms of help for children of one-parent families preferred by the Finer Committee (Finer Report 1974).

It is not only the children of working mothers, whether single parents or not, whose needs are unlikely to be met by nursery classes of the present kind. Many mothers who have big families or are otherwise under stress are unlikely to welcome part-day schooling, and few authorities seem like the ILEA to be markedly increasing the proportion of full-day places in difficult areas.

If disadvantaged children find places in nursery classes, will their day-to-day needs be better met and will they get a better educational start? There seems little doubt that they will be better looked after, not least because some relief to overburdened mothers may enable them to do more for their children in the rest of the day. As to the second question, research so far suggests some keys to success: involving parents in children's education as early as possible; a deliberate effort to strengthen children's use of language in an educational context; and a continuing and thoroughgoing attempt to improve their education over a longish period (Stenner and Mueller 1974; Halsey 1975b).

Right across the educational spectrum parents are beginning

to play a bigger part. Nursery schools were pioneers in welcoming parents, though the intention was more to help children to settle down than to accept their parents as powerful partners. The National Union of Teachers (NUT) has made clear its stock reservations. 'Teachers welcome parental support and are prepared to put their learning and experience at the disposal of parents. Nevertheless we see dangers in that it may be assumed that such community of interest confers an unqualified right upon parents to intervene in the educational function of the school as and when they see fit' (National Union of Teachers 1974). Though some exciting experiments are taking place, a major advance in teachers' attitudes is less likely when the profession is threatened by cutbacks and unemployment and teachers are inexperienced – as most are bound to be in the new nursery units.

As to children's language there are good grounds for hope in a research project which, in collaboration with 1,500 teachers to date (up to August 1975), first studied children's talk in school and is now looking at how it can be fostered. Help for the disadvantaged is one of the main purposes. Since the project covers the years from three to six, it satisfies one condition for success, an ongoing programme. It could also help indirectly by strengthening the links between nursery and primary teachers and so contributing to a common policy, made possible but by no means certain by the association of the new nursery classes with primary schools (Schools Council 1975).

Much of the most promising innovation is not in the main stream of nursery expansion. A variety of schemes for home visiting have, for example, been stimulated by the success of the West Riding EPA programme. Most begin with very young children. Increasingly, their main objective is not to influence children directly but to enable mothers to do more for their children both before and after they enter school. Some schemes have been initiated by voluntary bodies, some by local authorities; some use teachers, some lay members of the local community. Parental involvement is the strength also of the pre-school playgroup movement, welcomed and supported by some authorities, cold-shouldered by others. Though only 14% of playgroups cater for the children of manual workers in urban areas, 33% are in rural areas and among their children must be many who lack stimulus and companionship. Groups in rural areas and in poorer urban areas are increasing their number fastest. It is particularly encouraging that parents are more frequently involved in the poorer urban areas and in the country than elsewhere. Though playgroups in the poorer areas have more professional help than others, overall only 10% of playgroups have been visited by an education adviser from the local authority (Pre-school Playgroups Association 1975).

Nursery expansion was very untypical in one way. There was from the start a commitment to research which would monitor its effectiveness. Early in 1974 the DES set up a research management committee which began its work by identifying topics on which research was needed. In consequence there will be an enquiry into parental demand for education for the under fives, case studies of parents' involvement in it, and an investigation into the most effective ways of coordinating local services for the under fives. The Social Science Research Council also commissioned a research review on pre-school education which shocked and stimulated by its common sense view that child care and education – in the broadest sense – were indivisible. Among the more interesting outcomes is a three-year cross-disciplinary seminar, directed by Professor Bruner and associated with both the DES and the DHSS. It 'will look at how poverty affects children and on the other hand, what sort of thing gives a child a flying start' and 'different ways of intervening in families, communities and institutions to increase the support given to the pre-school child'. If the research does as well as it promises, there should be a good return when money for a second phase of expansion becomes available (Tizard 1975).

Raising the school-leaving age
If there is doubt whether the neediest are gaining from the now truncated expansion of nursery education, how have their older brothers and sisters fared from the extension of secondary school courses? As the newspapers filled with reports of part-time schooling it looked as though raising the school-leaving age had been a disaster. There were certainly shortages of teachers in some localities, and a more general one of specialists in mathematics and science and some practical subjects. But overall the teacher-pupil ratio in fact improved from 1:21.1 in 1973 to 1:20.5 in 1974 despite the addition of a third of a million

15-year olds (Department of Education and Science 1975a).

Even so, the raising of the school-leaving age was blamed for an increase in violence and truancy. As the time came for the first batch of pupils to complete their five-year course, the loss of confidence among educationists rose to a climax. It was summed up in a comment of Professor Judge that the raising of the school-leaving age was 'a mindless error which should be reversed at the earliest possible moment'. 'Beer for teachers' would, he suggested, have been a better way of raising educational standards.

A DES report has helped to restore perspective. Violence did seem to be increasing. The department has asked for information from local authorities and teachers' organisations about it and about such practices as suspension of pupils. How much disruption is due to the presence of an older age group is impossible to say. The report, based on inspectors' (HMI) contacts, said that amongst the 15-year olds it was confined to some areas and some schools and assessed the number of 15-year old dissidents as probably less than 10%. Truancy was widespread only in the summer term after examinations were over (Department of Education and Science 1975b). The decision has now been taken to end the term on the Friday before the spring holiday.

So much for the problems. What about the gains? The major advance seems to have been that a far higher proportion of students have followed individual programmes within a roughly common course and have retained to the end of their school career the expectation of some measurable success. Not expectation only. Between 1971-72 and 1973-74 there was a sharp rise of 5.5% in the number of those leaving school with one to four passes at O level. Even more remarkable, the percentage of those leaving without either GCE or CSE passes fell from 43.4% to 21% (Department of Education and Science 1975c). Admittedly, the minimum achievement suggested by these figures does not amount to very much. There are bound to be suggestions that the growth in the number of candidates has led to a fall in standards, though some safeguards against this are provided for. The boost to the enormous examination industry and the increasing amount of teacher time eaten up in it are hardly matters for satisfaction. Yet there is much to be said for schools which, granted the system, have given the great majority of their pupils an examination objective and have seen them succeed. Many teachers would prefer an all round pupil assessment but that is light years off.

In general RSLA schemes have almost certainly done a little towards making secondary school curricula and discipline more acceptable to those most likely to reject them. Linked courses, run in collaboration with colleges of further education and often making use of their practical facilities, are now run by three out of four local authorities. Provided they survive economy cuts, they should, in the long term, help to break down the absurd dissociation, at every level of administration and practice, between schools and further education, and make more likely a second chance for those who get least from conventional schooling.

Examination success there may be, but for many leavers it could lead only to unemployment and disillusion. There were 65,000 school leavers among the unemployed in October 1975. The situation would be a shade less serious if educational maintenance allowances and minor awards in further education had been reviewed. A larger number of boys and girls from poor families might then have continued to study full-time and improved their qualifications. In 1974 the Expenditure Committee of the House of Commons recommended that educational maintenance allowances for 16-18-year olds should be mandatory when families were in financial need, assessed on the same basis as eligibility for free meals. They suggested a national scale calculated on a formula derived from the Weaver Report of 1957. Allowances for students of the same age in school and further education were to be comparable in amount (House of Commons Expenditure Committee 1974). The DES carried out a fact-finding survey of local authority allowances in 1974 and in July 1975 a White Paper was promised (Hansard 11 July 1975).

Meantime, with melancholy repetition, each economy circular specified maintenance allowances as for no increase in spending. Authorities such as Liverpool, anxious to cater for large numbers of unemployed school leavers, have to organise courses which are part-time or short in duration and therefore do not disqualify their takers from unemployment or supplementary benefit. Other authorities which have cut further education may be even less able to help the unemployed.

Educational Priority Areas (EPAs)

Whenever the old issue is raised of concentrating on the disadvantaged, the first question is about definition. Who are the disadvantaged, and are they to be sought after in territories or in schools? The complexity is illustrated by the multifold patterns of deprivation which emerged from the Halsey research. The London team 'found that there were far more at risk children outside the EPA schools than in them' and urged that 'policies to assist disadvantaged schools or areas should not be seen as alternatives to policies which are focused on groups of children' (Halsey 1975a).

Whatever the problems of definition, the present government has certainly taken action. £11.8 million, later raised to more than £12 million, was made available to the Burnham Committee in June 1974 to raise the salaries of teachers in difficult schools at a time when pay generally was at a standstill. The Committee decided to award £275 a year to teachers who had been three years or more in a priority school, and £200 to the rest. The effect has been a substantial increase in pay for 11% of the profession. It is impossible to separate the impact of this allowance from that of the increase in the London allowance, from the major rise in salaries and boost to morale brought by the Houghton Report, and from the slow down in transfers resulting from the threat of teacher unemployment. The total effect is that mobility, which reached a peak in 1973, is now greatly reduced and difficult areas such as Newham,where 54% of teachers receive the allowance, seem to be adequately staffed. The new stability, though it too has its dangers, offers the best hope of anything that has happened in recent years for the improvement of schools in priority areas.

There has been little money available even for roofs over heads in 1974-75. Nevertheless, during 1974, £31 million was set aside in the 1974-75 programme for improving or replacing old primary schools in areas of special social need. In this way help has been given to some of the schools which lost their places in building programmes as a result of the economy cuts of 1973.

Just what local authorities are doing remains obscure. Teachers at the NUT conference urged that positive discrimination should take the form of additional teachers, building and equipment rather than differences in salary. Yet a spot enquiry made in some authorities with substantial numbers of social priority schools showed that several chose to distribute resources across the board. Part of the explanation probably lies in the fact that some authorities with severe problems have, for example, primary pupil/teacher ratios worse than the national average. Certainly authorities are unlikely to discriminate on a big scale unless like the ILEA they are in general spending above the average. Yet the evidence from abroad and from the ILEA itself is that little gain can be expected unless resources are heavily concentrated on the neediest. Even then success depends on a stable staff of good, experienced teachers (Inner London Education Authority 1974).

In 1974 the Secretary of State replied in a White Paper, *Educational Disadvantage and the Educational Needs of Immigrants*, to the Select Committee report of the previous year. The Committee had asked for an immigrant education advisory unit in the DES. The White Paper announced instead an Educational Disadvantage Unit, broadly concerned with all those, including different ethnic groups, suffering from educational disadvantage. Relatively little has been heard of the EDU which is an integral part of the DES and works under the same constraints. It may well have focused attention within the department on disadvantage and so contributed towards some of the measures which have been mentioned. Its public activities have consisted of the holding of a number of local seminars and of a national conference in preparation for the launching of an information centre on the education of the disadvantaged. This Educational Disadvantage Centre will be independent of the DES and of the Schools Council. Located in Manchester, it will come into full operation in 1976. Sir Alec Clegg, distinguished for his lifelong championship of the disadvantaged, is chairman of the management committee.

Coloured minorities

The government decision to approach the problems of immigrants as though they were no different from (or at any rate shared in the main with) others living in the older urban areas was in line with recent research which suggested that children's performance is affected more by social class and the quality of a school than by racial mix (Mabey 1975). It is too soon to judge how the Education Disadvantage Unit and the Education Disadvantage Centre will work out. Although immigrant interests are far from heavily represented on the Management Committee of the Centre, the teachers' unions have already suggested that too much emphasis has been placed on them.

The White Paper did of course accept (as it could not avoid doing) that newly established immigrants had specific needs and that many of those 'born here of all minority ethnic groups will experience continuing difficulties which must receive special attention from education service'. The difficulties of some of those born in England as well as abroad were shown by a recent study of multi-racial junior schools which stressed that poorer performance was characteristic even of 'those minority group children who had been judged in all probability not to be in need of special help with language' (Ewen *et al* 1975). In this and another recent enquiry by junior teachers in Bristol, the handicaps of West Indian children stand out as 'faced with highly specific problems of language, identity and race which need to be dealt with in a highly specific way . . . before the problem reaches crisis proportions in the secondary schools'.

To judge by such findings as these, the various measures to combat immigrant disadvantage described in the White Paper and in our 1974 report have had limited success. Responsibility for identifying those who need help now rests entirely with the local authorities. The DES failed to find any satisfactory way of producing regular statistics and discontinued them in January 1974. The major responsibility for action rests likewise with authorities though grants for extra staff continue to be available under the Local Government Act. The final figure for education expenditure under this act in 1973-74 was £11.8 million; the latest estimate for 1974-75 is £16.4 million. As with disadvantage generally, some authorities have thoroughgoing and detailed policies for support, while others do not.

Over the years help has also been available from the urban aid fund for authorities with high concentrations of immigrants. In 1974 bids were invited for grants from a special fund of £6 million which would, had circumstances been different, have gone as capital aid to president Amin of Uganda. Community centres in coloured areas, schemes for closer contact between homes and schools, language teaching for children and adults – in the neighbourhood and at work – received substantial help.

In the long run the outcome for coloured workers may depend at least as much on sensitive education for a multi-cultural society as on specific help for ethnic minorities. Teacher education is obviously important. A report on *Teacher Education for a Multi-cultural Society*, made at a time when teacher training was even more than usually in flux, stressed the need for redesigning courses to promote imaginative awareness of our new culture rather than adding extras. For those interested in working in multi-racial districts they suggested optional courses initially and above all in-service training (Community Relations Commission and Association of Teachers in Colleges and Departments of Education 1974).

Special education

At the end of 1973 the Conservative administration appointed a chairman, Mrs Mary Warnock, for the long hoped-for committee of enquiry into special education, in and out of special schools. The committee did not meet till September 1974. It was still receiving evidence at the end of 1975. In the meantime there have been advances. One of the more important gains from the Warnock committee may (as so often) be the stimulus given to officials to carry out long discussed reforms.

In the 1974 *Poverty Report* we described experiments in five authorities which were designed to test new ways of sorting out children's individual educational needs. Instead of assigning children to statutory categories, corresponding roughly to increasingly out-dated medical diagnoses, there was to be an all round descriptive profile, related to educational need. In 1975 this scheme, welcomed on all sides, was extended to the whole country. Parents are involved from the outset and, though doctors are too, recommendations are primarily educational.

DHSS statistics at the end of 1972 showed that 2,500 of the most severely deprived of all children, the mentally handicapped in hospital, were neither going to school nor having any education in their hospitals. A joint circular from the DES and the DHSS set out good practice, urging that whenever possible children should go out to special schools serving the community and that at the very least they should leave the ward or move to another part of it. (Department of Education and Science 1974b).

These children's problems are the most severe of all. The

biggest single group of children needing special education are the 'slow learners', often the victims of multiple deprivation, who are in ordinary primary and secondary schools. Many have learnt slowly but are in no real sense slow learners. The Bullock Report on literacy has pin-pointed some of their problems (Department of Education and Science 1975). Among the steps that could be taken to improve these children's prospects, two stand out. First, advisory remedial services in local authorities should be brought up to the level of the best – or at least to the average. Secondly – and not unrelated – these children, whose education is far cheaper than that of children in special schools, should be given a bigger share of resources in primary and secondary schools. Many schools have always shown great concern for them. But the current strains on comprehensive schools – a topic we have not touched on in this year's report – are great. Much of their energies and resources have, understandably, gone into striving to compete in examination success with selective schools.

The attitudes reflected in a recent pamphlet *When will they ever learn,* the report of a working party of secondary school heads, including many comprehensive heads, are most welcome. The working party was concerned with pupils who are physically, intellectually and socially handicapped. They committed themselves unequivocally to the need to distribute resources more evenly between the handicapped and the gifted. Dismayed by the small numbers of trained remedial teachers in secondary schools, they suggest that 'there must be a reappraisal by schools of the allocation . . . of money, accommodation, staffing and posts of responsibility'. Changes made 'may even mean a limitation of the range of subjects offered for example at sixth form level' (Association of Head Mistresses, Head Masters' Association 1975). The broad suggestions made are deeply compassionate – practical too since non-readers often turn into rowdies. Some of the details imply, as is clear too on a much wider front, the need for a close professional study of the problems of teaching children of mixed abilities, backgrounds and aspirations.

Adult literacy
In the past much confidence – now somewhat reduced – was placed in further education as an 'alternative route' to a variety

of educational goals. Here we are concerned with the adults whom schools have not even taught to read. Some idea of their extent was given by the large numbers of illiterates among conscripts during and after the last war, and among those committed to Borstal and prison. But it was not till the early seventies that voluntary bodies such as the British Association of Settlements focused attention on them. At the most conservative estimate there are 160,000 adults who cannot read as well as a seven-year old (British Broadcasting Corporation 1975). Figures of those who cannot read well enough for the ordinary business of living – to get or hold a job or to know what benefits they are entitled to – vary from one to two million. Estimates of the proportion who are getting any tuition range as widely. All agree it is a tiny minority. In 1973 48% of local authorities were not providing any literacy classes (Clyne 1973).

Following a conference of voluntary workers and local authorities in November 1973, the BAS published a policy document, *The right to read*. Its 17 proposals included one that 'the government must use its powers to direct the course and content of adult education to help local authorities to improve their facilities for illiterate adults. Local authorities cannot do a proper job on existing resources so we believe they should be supplemented by a special Adult Literacy Fund' (British Association of Settlements 1973).

In July 1974 the Secretary of State announced a once-only grant of £1 million. Though the amount was minute – perhaps one pound a head for the clients – the grant was novel enough. A new body, the Adult Literacy Agency, was set up to administer the fund and is to complete its work in 1976. Its funds are available to local authorities and to voluntary bodies. Though it cannot be used for paying the salaries of those responsible for literacy programmes in authorities and voluntary organisations, the single grant is being skilfully directed to bringing more than short-term benefits. Emphasis is being put on schemes to train paid and voluntary tutors and to train the trainers. Grants have been used to replace material intended for children with those for adults whose motives for reading lie largely in their work. The first issues of a paper written by literacy students have been subsidised. A telephone service has been manned to answer enquiries arising from a series of programmes the *BBC* is running. In autumn 1975 peak television time was being used to make non-readers realise that there were many others in the same predicament. Ten thousand requests for help were made in the first three weeks. Radio was also being employed to help train the large number of tutors needed.

The publicity and the grants have undoubtedly raised the amount and standard of provision. Every authority probably now has someone officially responsible for illiterates. Many authorities have excused literacy classes from the minimum numbers rule which binds other classes, and abolished or kept down fees. Some are using volunteers in association with paid tutors so that students can get individual help. Rather fewer have set going schemes similar to those pioneered by voluntary bodies for one-to-one help by volunteers, including teenagers teaching their contemporaries. Libraries are providing resources and in some instances a setting for tuition. The BAS have set up a three-year consultancy service for giving advice both to authorities and voluntary organisations. A National Committee for Adult Literacy has taken over from the BAS the responsibility of seeing that neither the government nor the public forget about illiteracy.

This amounts to substantial progress. But if the grant is not extended it may all come to an end. The Adult Literacy Resource Agency have submitted an interim report to the Secretary of State, asking for a further £1 million for the next three years. A continuing grant would enable, at this time of cut back, a full-time organiser to be appointed for each authority. In October 1975 the National Committee for Adult Literacy organised a conference intended amongst other things to persuade employers to play a part in the literacy campaign. Lord Crowther Hunt, the Minister for Higher Education, spoke warmly of what had been achieved and put out strong hints that the life of the Resource Agency would be prolonged and more money would be found for it (*The Times Educational Supplement* 1975).

Conclusion
The question was raised at the beginning of this chapter about the way in which education has weathered a period of extreme financial stringency. There is no doubt about the stringency.

The Barber budget was only the beginning, with things since then getting worse rather than better. The special budget of November 1974 allowed for an average increase in local authority expenditure on education of 4% in 1975-76. The DES expressed the hope that this would allow for the recruitment of newly-trained teachers and some improvements in staffing. But it became clear by the middle of 1975 that many authorities, heaving themselves out of the quagmire of reorganisation, had overspent in 1974 and were being forced into consequential cuts in 1975 over and above anything the government had done to them. Then in July 1975 the new Secretary of State gave warning that growth in 1976-77 would be limited in real terms to 2%, a figure that the authorities claimed would mean not any growth but actual cut backs. This in turn became out of date as the facts of overspending in 1975-76 became known. Standstill was the prospect for 1976.

The situation was not helped by the fact that the worst economy cuts since 1931 came at a time when the education lobby was, and is, particularly weak. The hold of the association of metropolican authorities (mainly Labour in politics) and of the association of county councils (mainly Conservative) is tight. The only national body, the Council of Local Education Authorities, can advocate; it cannot act without referring back to its parent bodies. Within the authorities education is vulnerable as the biggest spender. The rate support grant takes account of need but there are no strings as to how it is spent. The government and the authorities have on their side a falling population in primary schools and the prospect of a fall in secondary numbers. This is indeed a point that is taken up in the education section of the most recent economy circular which says that 'those authorities with a falling population, mainly large urban areas, should reduce their teaching staff proportionately'. Yet some of these areas are the very places where need is greatest and policy hitherto most inadequate.

It is unfortunately not possible to measure the outcome of the economies in terms of the distribution between richer and poorer. For that it would be necessary not just to review what has happened topic by topic, as we have been doing in this chapter, but locality by locality and school by school. Of that there is no tally. One investigation whose results were published during the year pointed to the need for fine differentiation (Byrne 1975). It showed how tenaciously old inequalities between authorities persist and, within them, old preferences for spending on the older and the abler pupils. The study concentrated on the policies of three authorities during the period 1945-65 and showed how difficult it was for authorities to plan at all when they were short of resources. Since 1965 the two 'poor' authorities have become 'poorer' as a result of reorganisation.

We cannot, because of the great variety of factors, be at all dogmatic about the general outcome. The tally, as we say, is not there. The root question for this whole book is also one for this chapter, that is whether in a period of contraction rather than expansion – in horizons as much as in cash – the distribution of resources has become more or less equal than it was. There are several reasons one might expect the answer to be less equal. At a time of expansion *extra* expenditure can to some extent, if the government so minds, be earmarked for the benefit of lower-income groups. Without too much protest more can be spent, for example, on schools and nurseries in poorer districts.

At a time of contraction such an emphasis may be more necessary than ever: the aim should be to economise at the expense of those who have most spent on them and as far as possible to leave untouched those who get least. This would mean deliberate redirection of resources between areas and also to younger age groups. Inequality in education is partly a matter of age. Each of the few who stay on into the sixth form, and, even more, the few who go on to university, cost annually a great deal more than younger children. In 1973-74 the cost for a university student was £1,049, that for a primary school child £140 and the university figure excludes loan charges and support for students (Hansard 27 October 1975). Redistribution down the age scale – however much it goes against the grain of the comprehensive reform – is also a redistribution from those who benefit most to those who benefit least.

References

Association of Head Mistresses and Head Masters, Association (1975) *When Will They ever Learn?*
British Association of Settlements (1973) *The Right to Read*

British Broadcasting Corporation (1975) *Handbook to Literacy*

Bullock Report (1975) *A Language for Life*, HMSO

E. Byrne (1974) *Planning and Educational Inequality*, National Foundation for Educational Research

P. Clyne (1973) *The Disadvantaged Adult*, Longmans

Community Relations Commission and Association of Teachers in Colleges and Departments of Education (1974) *Teacher Education for a Multi-cultural Society*

Department of Education and Science (1974a) *Educational Disadvantage and the Educational Needs of Immigrants*, HMSO

Department of Education and Science (1974b) *The education of mentally handicapped children and young people in hospital*, Circular 5/74, HMSO

Department of Education and Science (1975a) *Education and Science in 1974*, HMSO

Department of Education and Science (1975b) *Report on Education 83: The first year after RSLA*, HMSO

Department of Education and Science (1975c) *School Leavers: Provisional Figures for 1974*, press notice

Department of Education and Science (1975d) *Discovery of children requiring special education – the assessment of their needs*, Circular 2/75, HMSO

E. Ewen, C. Gibbs, R. Sumner (1975) *Language Proficiency in the Multi-racial Junior School*, National Foundation for Education Research

Finer Report (1974) *Report of the Committee on One-Parent Families*, HMSO

A.H. Halsey (ed.) (1975a) *Curriculum Innovation in London EPAs, Educational Priority vol. 3*, HMSO

A.H. Halsey (ed.) (1975b) *West Riding Project, Educational Priority, vol. 4*, HMSO

House of Commons Expenditure Committee (Education and Arts Subcommittee) (1974) Third report, *Educational Maintenance Allowances in the 16-18 Year Age Group*, HMSO

Inner London Education Authority (1974) *Education Committee Minutes*, 17 September 1974

Inner London Education Authority (1975) *Expansion of Nursery Education Programme*, Report by Education Officer to Education Committee, 29 October 1975

C. Mabey (1975) *Social and Ethnic Mix in Schools and the Relationship with Attainment of Children aged 8*, Centre for Environmental Studies

National Union of Teachers (1974) *The Provision of Pre-school Education in England and Wales 1974*

Pre-school Playgroups Association (1975) *Facts and Figures 1974*

Schools Council (1975) *Communication Skills in Early Childhood*, information sheet

A.J. Stenner and S.G. Mueller (1974) *A Successful Compensatory Education Model*, Phi Delta Kappan 55 246-8

The Times Educational Supplement (1975) 31 October 1975

B. Tizard (1975) *Early Childhood Education, A Review and Discussion of Research in Britain*, National Foundation for Educational Research

3 Perspectives

The context so far has been a national one. Charles Elliott takes a broader perspective and, starting with the world-wide inflation that has had such dramatic consequences inside Britain, examines its impact on the poorer countries of the world.

9 International inflation and international poverty

CHARLES ELLIOTT

Over the last three years, the international economy has been subjected to a triple shock of a kind and on a scale unprecedented in modern times. It is true that in general it has shown remarkable resilience, but that ought not to distract attention from the problems faced by those countries that contain the largest numbers of the poorest people on earth. Before I consider the effects of this shock, however, I need to examine its origins. This is the only way to understand its effects and judge the adequacy of the response of the international community in general and Britain in particular.

Origins of the triple crisis
It is a popular myth that the international inflation began with the quadrupling of the oil price in 1972-3. This is false. The oil crisis would certainly have caused serious problems to all oil-importing countries, but it is important to emphasise that a large group of countries was already facing major problems *before* oil prices were raised. Nearly every major industrialised country in the 'free' world reached a peak of economic activity in 1971-2. The result was a spectacular increase in the price of many raw materials and therefore an associated (though proportionately smaller) rise in the price of manufactured goods. We therefore have to distinguish carefully between those developing countries which benefited from the brief period of rapidly rising prices for their exports of primary products and those which either export no primary products or which export

products such as tea, which failed to share in the general price boom.

Among the former the receipts from the sale of primary products (the prices of some of which tripled or quadrupled in the space of three years) were for a brief period more than adequate to offset the steeply rising prices of manufactured goods from the developed countries. Among the latter there was no such temporary respite: indeed, countries such as Bangladesh, Pakistan, India, Sri Lanka, Kenya, Uganda and Ethiopia found that they were paying substantially more, not only for manufactured imports from the industrialised countries, but also for such primary commodities as they imported.

There is a further distinction that is important in this connection and one that is seldom adequately emphasised in the literature. During the boom in the industrialised countries in the early 1970s, world trade expanded rapidly. The exports of processed and semi-processed goods from the poor countries into the rich countries increased fast. From the point of view of the poor countries, this is a particularly significant component of foreign trade, since processed and semi-processed products not only bring in more foreign exchange but also create more jobs in the poor countries. Increased world demand for this group of products therefore reduces directly the burden of urban (and possibly rural) poverty. During this period, then, those poor countries which had so far advanced their industrialisation that they were exporting sizeable quantities of manufactures or semi-manufactures experienced a short period when they could both expand employment and earn additional foreign exchange to meet the rising costs of all classes of imports.

We therefore have a threefold classification of the poor countries. First, there were primary producers which benefited from the boom in the prices of those products. Second, there were those countries which had established an export-oriented industrial sector which benefited from the rising demand for imports in the rich countries. Among these one could include Taiwan, South Korea, Hong Kong, Malaysia, Brazil and to a rather lesser extent Uruguay and Argentina. The third group constitutes those countries locked into the export of products which do not respond much to rapid industrial growth in the rich countries – the products which have a low income elasticity of demand. The classic examples of these are the countries of the Indian subcontinent, exporting products such as tea and jute and a very limited range of industrial products. Since these countries are heavily dependent upon imports for food, industrial goods and many raw materials (including fertiliser), their balance of payments is always precarious – and politically sensitive. Even if the other two components of the triple shock had not broken upon them in 1973 and 1974, economic growth and political stability were already seriously jeopardised by circumstances over which the governments of these countries had no control.

But it was the other two components of the triple shock that raised these problems to nightmare proportions. Seen through the eyes of most grass-roots politicians, the full horror of the nightmare stemmed more from the acute shortage of food than from the high cost of oil. For in every poor country more people are more concerned about food than about petrol.

In 1971 the international price of wheat was $62 (approximately £30) per ton. By 1973 it had reached $139 (approximately £68) a ton and by January 1974 it had risen to a staggering $214 (approximately £105) per ton. The explosion in the price of rice (in some ways a more sensitive food grain than wheat in the developing countries of South East Asia) was even more dramatic. In 1971 the price was $179 (approximately £88) per ton. By March 1974 it had reached a record $603 (approximately £295) a ton – nearly a five-fold increase in two and a half years.

I do not have the space here to describe in detail the causes of this upward leap in the price of the world's food supply. Needless to say, long-term and short-term causal factors were both at work. Amongst the former were not only the continued increase in world population (which, despite much current alarmist comment, is probably not a major factor); the continuing failure of agricultural policy in most of the developing countries to increase food production at an adequate pace; rising urban incomes in some developing countries which has greatly increased the demand for high quality foodstuffs; and the rising demand for food grains in the rich countries for use as animal feeds. Amongst the short-run causes, the most important was the poor harvests in most of the major food growing areas of the world, which led to substantial shipments of food grains to Russia and to a lesser extent to China and the consequent elimination of grain reserves in Canada, America, Australia and (though quantitively much less significant) Latin America.

As on average 14% of developing countries' total imports are foodstuffs, it is easy to see that a rapid rise in prices can add greatly to their balance of payments difficulties. Nor is this all. Because grains were being sold to Russia and other developed countries, there was less available to give away as food aid. In 1970-72 India had received an annual average 1.8 million metric tons. In 1973 she received no more than 52,000 metric tons. For all developing countries (except Pakistan for which data are not available) there was a shortfall in food aid in 1973 of 6.6 million metric tons.

Notice that the countries already identified as those being at the greatest disadvantage as a result of the boom in primary product prices and the associated inflation of the rich countries are also the countries affected most severely by the physical shortage and high prices of important food grains. The four major countries of the Indian subcontinent are all food importers. In India, severe drought had greatly increased reliance on food imports at a time that could hardly have been less opportune. In Bangladesh the same was broadly true: severe flooding combined with the near breakdown of internal administration made the need for food imports particularly acute but the difficulties of distribution virtually insoluble. In Sri Lanka, acreage planted to rice slumped as government pre-election promises to cancel peasants' debts were broken. The government therefore found itself with the double burden of importing food and maintaining its much criticised policy of distributing free food to low income earners. The more publicised disasters in the Sahel and Ethiopia at least had the effect of generating wide public and half-hearted political concern at a problem that could not be expected to disappear overnight even in the best of all Panglossian worlds.

None the less both the primary commodity/industrial inflation and the world food crises could arguably be presented as relatively short term. It was highly improbable that the primary commodity boom would continue for long; and there was some evidence that the rising political determination in industrial countries to control domestic rates of inflation would begin to pay off and would ultimately (perhaps with rather a long lag) be reflected in a levelling off of export prices. Similarly, despite much public hysteria dutifully orchestrated by the UN Food and Agriculture Organisation (FAO), there was a better-than-ever chance that virtually world-wide poor harvests would be followed by world-wide good harvests and a resultant collapse in the inflated international price of food grains. Widespread changes in agricultural policy in both rich and poor countries (the main impact of which was to pass higher prices back to the farmer and thus stimulate increased production) was a long-overdue step which made it probable that, given reasonably good climatic conditions, world food production would in the middle term increase fast and rebuild stocks to an adequate level.

But with the third component of the triple shock – the quadrupling of oil prices – such modest optimism was impossible. For the circumstances of the oil revolution showed clearly that the fragile unity of both the Organisation of Petroleum Exporting Countries (OPEC) and the Organisation of Arab Petroleum Exporting Countries (OAPEC) was political and not economic. The elaborate models of oil production and consumption which had been so laboriously built in both the United States and France to show that an oil producers' oligopoly could never survive were shown to be misconceived. With the rapid expansion of investment in the North Sea and other high cost producing areas in and around North America, Southern Africa and the Pacific Basin, it had become clear by late 1974 that, despite falling demand and rising world production, a price of over $9 a barrel would be maintained – if necessary by some of the Arab oil producers curtailing production.

Further, by mid 1975 it had become clear that one of the highest priorities of the OPEC countries – namely to peg the price of oil to the price of goods they import from the rich countries – was unstoppable. High oil prices are here to stay.

Like planners in the rich countries, economists in the poor countries had assumed that oil would continue to be cheap relative to other sources of energy. Like the rich countries they therefore found themselves in a very exposed position when that assumption was proved ill-founded. Much electric power is derived from oil. Much agricultural technology is heavily oil-dependent both in a direct sense (for example, through the

use of tractors and motor-driven hand cultivators) and indirectly through the adoption of new strains of seeds (the so called
miracle varieties), one of the chief characteristics of which is
high responsiveness to the application of chemical fertilisers
that derive from oil.

In this sense the impact of the oil revolution far transcends
the balance of payments effect, serious though this last is. In
Uruguay, for instance, the revolution in oil prices added 39%
to the import bill; in India, it added 24% and in Pakistan 16%.
This certainly presented an unforeseen and massive problem to
the oil-importing countries of the Third World. Given international cooperation and statesmanship of a high order, it was
arguably a handleable problem.

But it was, and still is, hard to see how countries heavily
committed to mechanised and fertiliser-dependent agriculture
can adjust to a situation in which the basic inputs become
increasingly expensive (by an order currently running at about
30% a year), without making food in those countries so expensive that the great bulk of those who buy it in both rural and
urban areas will simply be unable to afford it. The demands
that these countries abandon their current level of agricultural
technology, and return to animal-powered organic farming,
demands sometimes heard from those concerned with the
long-run ecological impact of systems of 'high' farming, are for
the most part romantic nonsense. Even if implementable, they
would imply not only a drastic fall in yields and therefore in
rural incomes but also a huge fall in total production and
therefore a serious aggravation of the basic problem of food
supply. The current interest in intercropping with legumes and
improving the genetic stock of neglected 'indigenous' crops like
cassava are two important steps in this direction.

Changes within countries
So far I have discussed this triple shock to the poor countries at
the national level. What happened at the subnational level?
Within these 'most severely affected' countries, which groups
have really paid the costs of the triple shock of the primary
product industrial goods inflation, the world food crisis and the
oil crisis?

There can be no doubt that this triple shock has imposed
upon these countries the need to reduce consumption on a huge

scale. In Sri Lanka, for example, the *additional* costs of oil and foodstuff imports in 1974 amounted to 14% of national incomes. The critical question then is: whose consumption has been (and is likely to continue to be) reduced?

I shall look in turn at each of the three components – imported manufactures, imported oil and imported food.

The rise in the price of imported manufactures is unlikely to be felt directly by the poor. They do not typically buy cars, refrigerators, air conditioning plants and the other knick-knacks of western civilisation. These goods are bought by the highly privileged urban groups, many of whom are in a strong position to defend their standard of living by demanding wage and salary increases or by raising the price of the services they supply.

But in that way there may be significant *indirect* effects upon the poor. Take, for instance, the case of teachers. Teachers tend to be well organised and able to defend their standard of living better than most other groups in most developing countries. Further, their salaries constitute a large part (sometimes as much as 75%) of the total cost of the educational service. If teachers demand an increase in their money wages, governments tend to finance that increase by reducing the quantity and/or quality of education provided. They reduce the quantity by building and staffing fewer schools; they reduce the quality by making classes bigger and diluting the quality of staff. In either case it is the less privileged groups, particularly the rural poor, who are likely to suffer most from this cut back. For it is they who are least well served by schools, they who tend to be the first victims of lower standards in teaching service.

But the imports of manufactured goods into poor countries are not comprised only of consumer goods. The majority of manufactured imports are capital goods – lathes, drills, turbines, cranes and process plant. What is the effect upon the urban poor of a reduction in the imports of such capital goods implied by the balance of payments problems of the most severely affected countries?

At this point one needs to be careful. For it is by no means as self evident as is sometimes assumed that a reduction in the availability of these capital goods will have an adverse effect on the living standards of the urban poor – at least in any but the very longest run. For the importation of some types of capital goods is, from the point of view of the urban poor, a very mixed blessing. It may make the total output of goods grow faster. It may modernise productive methods. It may conceivably (though improbably) improve the quality and reduce the price of items that are widely consumed. But it may also pose a real threat to the employment of handworkers and unskilled labourers and it may (especially in the short run) lead to a further concentration of income in the hands of those who own the factories or capital goods, and those with relatively high skills (the managers, secretaries and mechanics) employed by them.

The effect of the cancellation of a new factory to produce cotton shirts may be to reduce the demand for managers and a few skilled machinists; but it may also be to deliver from the near certainty of unemployment hundreds of backroom tailors currently supplying the market at which the factory is aimed.

Oil

As I have already shown, even in some of the poorest countries the additional oil bill was a frightening proportion of total imports. In Ethiopia, one of the poorest countries in the world, the 1974 oil bill was a quarter of *all* imports. Who paid for this? The most obvious answer is those who consume the oil either directly (for example, by buying petrol for their cars) or indirectly by buying products in the manufacture of which oil is a major input, eg plastics and petrochemicals. Again most of these goods are not widely bought outside the urban elite: goods consumed by the poor use so little oil either directly or indirectly that a rise in the price of oil makes little difference. One immensely important exception already mentioned is fertilisers. Who pays then for an increase in the cost of fertilisers – the producer or the consumer?

Most farmers have been able to pass the higher cost of fertilisers back to the consumer. Even in those countries in which governments try to regulate the price of food – even manipulate it in favour of the urban consumer (for example the Philippines and Sri Lanka), the scale of the price changes and the coincidence of the world food crisis with the oil crisis have ensured that producer prices of food have been raised substantially – usually by more than enough to offset the increase in fertiliser prices.

There can be little doubt, then, that within the most seriously affected countries the groups bearing the brunt of the implied fall in consumption are (i) urban low income earners in the informal sector (ii) rural producers who are dependent upon oil-based inputs and (iii) 'marginal' consumers of social services who are squeezed out as a result of restrictive government expenditure on the services in question. To some extent of course the third group may coincide with either the first or second. Almost by definition the third group are poor, ill-educated, ill-adjusted to the social situation in which they find themselves and lacking either the social skills or political leverage to protect their 'social wage'.

The rich countries

What has been the response of the rich countries to the triple shock so far described? Although in the light of the analysis in the rest of this volume it is unnecessary to labour the point, it is worth repeating that the rich countries no less than the poor suffered from each of the three components of that shock. They were obliged to pay much higher primary commodity prices. They found themselves in the grip of an externally induced but domestically reinforced inflation. They, or at least the food importers amongst them (of which the UK is a leading example) had to pay much higher prices for imported food and feedstuffs. Supremely they were much more vulnerable to the oil price revolution than were the great majority of developing countries. Although it is true that in absolute terms the rich countries became much poorer, it is also true that for the first time since 1930 the rich countries were collectively faced with the prospect (which is still in the process of being realised) of a drastic and sustained fall in living standards accompanied by historically high levels of unemployment.

Under these circumstances, it would be unrealistic, however desirable, to look for major gestures of goodwill or generosity towards the developing countries in general and the most seriously affected among them in particular. It would be much more in accord with the Realpolitik of international economic relations for rich countries to try to secure their supplies of primary products and to insulate themselves from the worst effects of the oil crisis.

That is precisely what they are doing.

The rich countries were badly shaken, first, by the speed and extent of the price boom in primary products (with some prices more than doubling in twelve months) and, secondly and perhaps more forcefully, by the display of strength by OPEC even after a sharp turndown in world demand for oil.

Most impressive (and threatening) of all was the coalescence of these two features in the growing solidarity of the oil producers with the rest of the Third World (emphasised by the Algiers conference in early 1975 and the Special Session of the UN six months later). However unreal talk of 'producer power' may seem, and however diverse the political objectives of the participants in the Algiers conference, the threat is clear enough. With the huge wealth now controlled by the oil producers, allied with the control of primary products in the hands of a number of countries basically favourable to Arab aspirations in the Middle East, the prospect of an alliance that could shift the centre of economic power decisively away from the rich countries of the North Atlantic has now to be taken with the utmost seriousness.

It has been. Over the last 18 months the rich countries, both collectively and individually, have made a series of attempts to convince primary producers in general and the oil producers in particular of their bona fides as 'partners in development' and of the essentially harmonious (or at least harmonisable) interest of producers and consumers in securing the maximum cooperation to expand the world economy.

This sudden conversion has necessarily demanded some embarrassing U-turns. Having opposed commodity agreements in principle, and sabotaged at least three in practice, the Americans are now urging them as a high priority. Having played an inglorious role at UN Conferences on Trade and Development (UNCTADs) II and III, the British government has already opened the bidding for UNCTAD IV by announcing the outlines of an ambitious plan to secure supplies of essential primary products from Commonwealth countries in exchange for price and market guarantees. Having in the past dismissed the demands of the developing countries as 'ill-timed', 'shrill' and 'unreasonable', the British Government (in common with almost every other industrial power) is now falling over itself to assure primary commodity producers that it wishes to be both an architect of and a party to any 'new economic order' that will give lasting expression to a co-operation between primary commodity producers and consumers.

How far is this 'me-tooism'? How far is it an attempt to buy time to see how real is the alliance of interest between the rich, highly organised oil producers on the one hand and the less rich and largely disorganised primary producers on the other? How far is it a smokescreen, put out to disguise EEC/US man-oeuvres to smash the oil cartel and any putative imitators of that example? These are questions that need to be asked but are extraordinarily difficult to answer at this time. There are however one or two straws in the wind that may be relevant though, as we shall see, they tend to give contradictory indications of the way the wind is blowing.

One such straw is the Lomé Convention, signed with much international brouhaha between the enlarged European community on the one hand and 46 African, Carribbean and Pacific states on 28 February 1975. Revealingly, François-Xavier Ortoli, President of the Commission of the European Community, greeted the signature of the Lomé Convention with these words: 'The community must commit itself wherever possible to cooperation based on the search for long-term economic interdependence. . . . It is possible to ensure the difficult birth of a new world order through cooperation, not confrontation' (*Courier* 1975).

Although the negotiations that culminated in the Lomé convention began long before any of the components of the triple shock emerged, the convention none the less became invested with a special significance in the light of that triple shock. It was presented to the world as the forerunner of a new world economic order in which the self interest of the industrial countries would be pursued with a greater degree of enlightenment, a longer time horizon and a more generous spirit of cooperation than has been the normal character of the economic relations between the rich and the poor in the post-war period.

How far is this image of the Lomé convention justified by the facts? The first point to remember is that although the African Commonwealth and Pacific (ACP) countries number 46, most of them are small and heavily dependent on the economies of the EEC. By far the largest of the ACP countries is Nigeria which, with a population of nearly 80 million, comprises more than half the total population of the 22 Comonwealth countries included in the convention.

Secondly, few of the countries involved are in any significant sense competitive with the EEC in terms of either agricultural or industrial production. Because the great bulk of them are ex-colonies of either France or Britain, their economies have developed along complementary lines. To this extent 'inter-dependence', one of the key words of the convention rhetoric, is built in. The really tough issues of access to protected markets for manufactured products (especially textiles, leather goods, hand tools, ceramics, enamel ware and other sensitive areas) and competitive temperate zone agricultural products, were avoided. It is not insignificant that the negotiators found the problem of sugar (in the context of the renewal or re-negotiation of the Commonwealth Sugar Agreement) by far the most contentious issue, satisfactorily settled only at the last moment. Negotiations with competitive Latin American producers of temperate agricultural products or competitive South East Asian producers of manufactured goods would have proved very much more difficult. To put it more crudely than the facts fully justify, the EEC does not find it difficult to be generous when the costs of such generosity are small and distant.

If the list of participants looks like Hamlet without the Prince of Denmark, and the access terms like Macbeth without the blood, the real interest in Lomé lies in STABEX, the device designed to stabilise the export earnings of the ACP countries. It is beyond my scope here to review STABEX in detail: critiques are readily available elsewhere. (Overseas Development Institute 1975).

The main points can be quickly made. First, it is a relatively small scheme in terms of the financial outlays involved and it is supposed to be largely (though not wholly) self-financing. Secondly, the distribution of benefits from STABEX is determined by the pattern of ACP exports: this is not consistent with a need-determined distribution. Third, and in some ways most revealing, only one mineral export is concerned – iron ore – and that only after the most bitter conflict. The Community made it clear that it 'remains firmly opposed to mineral products being included under the system' – for to include them would be to deny to the Community the long-run benefit of new, low-cost sources already projected.

How far is the Lomé convention a first step, a pioneering effort which will eventually be replaced by a larger convention covering some of those countries currently excluded, offering more generous terms of access (particularly for agricultural commodities) and extending the STABEX principle to cover a much wider range of primary products?

It is in this context that the extremely cool response accorded Harold Wilson's ideas on collaboration between primary producers and consumers at the 1975 Commonwealth Conference needs to be seen. There can be little doubt that the primary producing countries will in future hold out for both more generous and more comprehensive treatment than they were able to secure at Lomjyxjxem In this respect the contrast that was drawn Zparticularly by EEC propagandistsz between the collaboration of the Lomjyxjxe Convention on the one hand and the confrontation between the oil producers and the industrialised West on the other is over simplistic. In future there will surely be jebothjx confrontationje andjx collaborationm The confrontation will be used as a tool to ensure that the collaboration is as favourable as possible (or perhaps as little prejudicial as possible) to the primary producers first, and the Third World in general second. Any new Lomé convention will have to take into account (in a way that at bottom Lomé does not) that the balance of economic power is shifting – fast.

What about the reaction of the rich countries in general and Britain in particular to the second component of the triple shock, namely the 'world food crisis'? Here one needs to differentiate carefully between the short-run reaction to the public and international hysteria focused by the World Food Congress, and the longer term issues about what an industrialised country can in fact do to help ensure an adequate global food supply and the distribution of that food in a remote Third World country.

As far as the short run goes there is little ground for complacency. The British participation in the World Food Congress of 1974 was one of the least glorious episodes in the history of British diplomacy. The only major British initiative was to offer 25,000 tons of fertiliser to the special pool created by the FAO for distribution to countries most seriously affected by the shortage and high cost of fertiliser – a mean-spirited offer that richly deserved the howls of protest that it drew from the aid lobby both within and outside Parliament. The offer was subsequently increased to 100,000 tons – still a 'drop in the ocean of need', in the words of the Minister of Agriculture, but, given the high import cost of fertiliser (around 60%) and the additional grant under the India Aid agreement to finance 145,000 tons of fertiliser imports for India, at least a less parsimonious reaction of a government that in 1973 had published with considerable satisfaction a report on 'British aid and the relief of malnutrition'.

Further, an increase in the British contribution to the World Food Programme from £1.5 millions in 1974 to over £8 millions in 1975 and an increase in the British share of EEC food aid also helped, if late in the day, to correct the initial reluctance of the British government to take the world food crisis seriously.

If the short-term reaction of the British government to the world food crisis has been unhappy – an unhappiness stemming in part from the division of responsibility between the Foreign and Commonwealth Office, the Ministry of Overseas Development and the Ministry of Agriculture – the longer-term reaction is more promising. In her brief but immensely creative period at the Ministry, Judith Hart set in train a major policy overhaul which, if implemented by her successor, is likely greatly to increase the proportion of British aid going to the rural poor. This overhaul did not arise directly out of the world food crisis: its intellectual roots go analytically deeper and chronologically further back.

The cynical may say this is the new orthodoxy, currently adopted by the World Bank, the US Agency for International Development (USAID), the Canadian International Development Agency and the Swedish International Development Authority. So it is. But that does not make it any the less relevant, refreshing or potentially revolutionary. For as Judith Hart herself made clear, an important criterion by which applications for British aid will in future be judged is the participation of rural people in their own development.

To succeed in the rural development process which can help the peasants of the world they must themselves participate in it. They must be involved: involved in the decisions made about the development of the land they farm, involved in the decisions about the villages, involved in determining the planning priorities which affect their lives. Success in rural development . . . depends on the full participation of the people (Hart 1975).

That perception implies official recognition by the British government that aid that reinforces oppressive or authoritarian structures and institutions in the rural areas is counterproductive. Projects and programmes are acceptable only if set in a rural environment in which the poor assume increasing responsibility for their own destiny. This in turn implies that in future (again if her successor is faithful to Judith Hart's vision) British aid will be deliberately biased in favour of those governments which, at national level, give a high priority to popular participation in rural development.

To these criteria and to this bias Judith Hart committed the British Government at the Commonwealth meeting on food production and rural development in February 1975. It is hard to overemphasise how far this advances official British aid strategy. In political terms, Judith Hart herself saw it as a direct attack upon the politics of neo-colonialism. In economic terms, it was seen as an attempt to give greater emphasis to the distribution of income even if (perhaps temporarily) at the expense of the growth of national incomem Administrativelyn it was an attempt to wean at least some signil£cant part of British aid away from the deadening influence of the Foreign and Commonwealth Office.

I now turn to the third component of the triple shock: the oil crisis. What has been the reaction of the rich countries in general and Britain in particular to this aspect of the triple shock? Certainly there was some modest increase in the commitments of aid to the countries hardest hit by oil prices both bilaterally and through the various agencies of the UNm Less publicised but perhaps more significant in the long run was the announcement that from October 1o7tn aid to those developing countries which had a gross national product per head below US $200 would be on grant rather than on loan terms. This represents a further softening of British aid which in future will make an appreciable difference to the real value of British aid to the poorest countries – among which are those most seriously affected by the oil crisis.

It is not part of my argument to belittle or condemn these improvements in the British aid effort, though the grant element of British aid is still less than average for all Organisation for European Economic Cooperation (OECD) countries. But they pale into insignilacance by contrast with the negative impact that Britain has had on the developing countries through her determination to lanance her balance of payments delacit with bilateral borrowing from the oil rich countriesmfsjxThis is so important that it deserves a word of explanation. As is now widely appreciated, the raising of the oil price has led to the accumulation of large surpluses in the hands of nearly all the major oil producers. Simultaneously it has led to oil importers, both rich and poor, running large and in many cases quite unprecedented balance of payments deficits. Some countries have been able to reduce those deficits relatively rapidly (eg Japan and Germany): other countries, amongst them most of the poorest, have found it impossible to incease the value of their exports much in a time of declining world demand. They are therefore faced with large and semi-permanent balance of payments deficits.

Two questions then arise. First, what will the oil-rich countries do with their accumulated surpluses? Secondly, how will those countries with semi-permanent balance of payments deficits finance them? In the best of all humane worlds the obvious solution would be for the oil-rich countries to lend to the countries with balance of payment deficits. But of course the world does not work like that. Although the oil producers have shown themselves much more generous in giving aid than the rich countriesjeIjxmore than three times as generous as a proportion of Gross National Product ZGNPzjeIjxthe bulk of their funds has been invested in London and New Yorkn with a small but increasing proportion in Paris and Frankfurtm There are good technical reasons for thismfsThe British and American capital markets arè the largest and most sophisticated in the world. The oil countries have had long historical association with these markets. Their financial advisers are based there. And sterling and the dollar are still major trading currencies. This has meant that, while the rich countries have been able to finance their balance of payments deficits, the poor countries have not.

Particularly regrettable has been the fact that neither the British nor American governments have shown any enthusiasm for the various schemes which would allow the oil producers to lend their surpluses to international agencies like the International Monetary Fund (IMF) or the World Bank which could then lend to the countries most in need of this kind of support. The official counter-argument – that the oil producers do what they want with their own funds and the fact that they choose to put them in London is no more than a convenient coincidence – is hardly convincing. Certainly the oil producers have shown little enthusiasm for such IMF schemes as have been floated but such schemes have been robbed of the necessary allurements – for example, high interest rates, security, flexibility and multi-currency denomination – at the insistence of the beneficiary countries of the current pattern of recycling.

Certainly an international scheme that would attract surpluses could be produced: but neither the British nor the Americans want such a scheme. So far they have been able to prevent it and thereby have managed to attract between 55% and 75% of the oil surpluses to insulate them from the worst effects of the current recession. It is not insignificant that in the late summer of 1975 the American and British seemed to be entering a period of interest rate warfare in an attempt to maintain their hegemony of the market for surplus petro-dollars. However grave the internal economic situation of Britain, it is quite certain that it would have been immeasurably worse if we had not succeeded in borrowing such huge sums. But our success in this respect is the failure of the international financial institutions – and therefore of the poorest and most vulnerable of the world. Never has the protection of our own affluence been more immediately at the cost of the deepening poverty of the poor.

Summary

This rapid survey of the British response to the triple shock suffered by the poor countries, in particular the poorest people in those poor countries, inevitably reveals a mixture of good intention, half-heartedness and self interest. We seem to be in a twilight period when the full implications of the shift in the balance of economic power are still being digested, not only in

Whitehall but in the developing countries themselves. There can be little doubt that a new deal for the poor countries and perhaps the poorest among them will be extracted from whatever government happens to be in power. The days of British largesse to the Commonwealth and political trafficking to the rest of the Third World are rapidly drawing to an end. The next few years will see the negotiation of comprehensive agreements that cover the entire waterfront of economic relations between the rich and the poor.

The only choice before us will be whether we negotiate those agreements willingly, collaboratively and cheerfully or whether they are forced upon us by the use of the immense financial leverage that has already passed to those whom, ten years ago, we treated with a typical mixture of disdain and paternalism.

References

Courier (1975) no.31, March 1975

J. Hart (1975) 'The priority for rural development overseas' Speech to Royal Society of Arts, 6 May 1975

Overseas Development Institute (1975) *The Lomé Convention: ODI Briefing Paper*, March 1975

This account of two studies in Paris and London shows some of the differences and similarities in the lives of the poor – and their better-off neighbours – in the two places. It suggests in particular the crucial role that housing policy can play.

10 Deprivation in Paris and London
PETER WILLMOTT and PIERRE AIACH

Last year's *Poverty Report* described a cross-national comparison, in which data about poverty were drawn from small-scale surveys in Dortmund and London. In his introduction to the *Report*, Michael Young expressed the hope that more such studies would be mounted in the future. The case remains a powerful one. If, in cross-national comparative studies, differences in social policy and administrative structure can be related to the day-to-day experience of samples of populations, nations will be able to learn from each other. Britain's continuing membership of the EEC (confirmed in June 1975), together with the expressed desire of member countries for 'harmonisation' of their social policies, offers an opportunity to cooperate on such comparisons with its immediate neighbours in Europe, and to put the findings to good use

Comparative studies should, in our view, include regular nation-wide surveys of poverty. During 1976 the Institute of Community Studies hopes, in cooperation with research institutes in France and Western Germany, to take further the earlier pilot work and later move on to national surveys in the three countries. If all goes well, such nation-wide surveys will eventually be taken over by governments and extended to other countries in the EEC and beyond. But, in addition to surveys of that kind, we see a role for a series of smaller-scale comparisons, concentrating on the needs of particular sections of the population, such as the disabled, the old, large families, or residents of various kinds of 'deprived' district.

The two studies

In this chapter we report in the meantime on two local studies of inner city areas, one in Paris and the other in London. For various reasons the studies could not be designed jointly, so that we cannot for the most part draw direct statistical comparisons between them, but there were some similarities of purpose and methods, and we can draw upon the two studies to suggest at least some broad conclusions.

The Paris research was undertaken for the French government (Commissariat Général du Plan). We – a British and a French sociologist – collaborated on it, and the research was carried out by the medico-social division of the Institut National de la Santé et de la Recherche Médicale (INSERM). It was started in 1973 and completed in 1975 (Aiach 1975).

The study set out to explore, in the context of a particular district, the processes of what in French is called 'cumulative inequality'. We first chose our district in Paris – one with a large proportion of poor residents but also with some who were better off. We then tried to get to know as much as we could about the selected *quartier*, Folie Mericourt, and its institutions, and we carried out lengthy (mostly tape-recorded) interviews with 138 parents (couples or lone mothers) who had at least one child aged 16 or under. We chose this stage in life rather than another because we were interested in the influence upon the second generation of cumulative inequality.

This last phrase is clearly the gallic equivalent of 'multiple deprivation', the difference being that the English term deals only with people at the bottom end of the various distributions, whereas the French is broader, taking into account accumulations of privilege as well as of deprivation.

The interest in multiple deprivation figured as part, but only part, of the study in London; this was in an area in Lambeth which had been selected as containing a range of characteristic inner city problems. The Lambeth study had much wider terms of reference than that in Paris. Like similar studies in Liverpool and Birmingham, it was intended to take a comprehensive look at inner city problems, combining research and small-scale action projects in such a way as 'to provide a base for general conclusions on policies and action' (Department of the Environment 1974a). This study, started in 1973 and due to end in 1976, is being carried out by a joint team from the

Shankland Cox Partnership, architects and town planners, and the Institute of Community Studies.

To contribute to the Lambeth study as a whole, the team carried out, at an early stage, a sample survey of 900 households and 1,600 individual adults. The survey covered the general population in the study area; its methods are described and some of the main findings reported elsewhere (Department of the Environment 1974b).

On the subject of multiple deprivation in particular, an interim report has already been published (Department of the Environment 1975a) and some further work was in hand when this chapter went to press. Whereas the Paris research concentrated on families with children, that on multiple deprivation in Lambeth was concerned with the whole population. Various forms of statistical analysis were carried out on the original sample survey and some families were re-interviewed more intensively. For the purpose of comparison with Folie Mericourt, we have been able to draw on the original sample interviews with households containing children aged 16 or under (314, or about a third of the sample), and on the 30 or so intensive interviews with families who had children and were also deprived.

The starting point of the Lambeth statistical analysis was to select a number of indices of deprivation, so as to see how often such deprivations 'overlapped' and in what kinds of household. After various preliminary rounds with longer lists, the analysis settled on six deprivations – income, having a car and/or telephone, overcrowding, housing amenities, disability and employment instability. With each, a 'cut-off' point was selected below which a household was judged to be deprived. That for income, for instance, followed the procedure used in the surveys of poverty in Bethnal Green and Camden described in previous *Poverty Reports;* households were counted as financially deprived if their income was below their supplementary benefit entitlement plus 20%. Likewise, a household was regarded as deprived in terms of housing amenities if it had exclusive use of less than four out of a standard list (bathroom, sink, washbasin, hot water, WC, kitchen, garden). This procedure was extended, in the light of the Paris experience, to include measures of 'privilege' as well as deprivation. A household was, for instance, regarded as privileged in housing amenities if it had all seven amenities on the list.

Although both studies were intended to be of inner city areas containing concentrations of deprivation, there were some important differences. Folie Mericourt was chosen as containing some of the worst housing in Paris, while the area selected in Lambeth was supposed to be not so much an extreme case as a place including examples of characteristic inner city problems.

Contrasted families

To illustrate what cumulative inequality means in the context of the Paris *quartier*, we can compare the circumstances and lives of two families in our study, one relatively privileged and the other relatively deprived. The names we give are fictitious.

M. Boursault, aged 39, was the marketing director of a large multi-national company. His salary was 7,000 francs a month; his firm paid him a further 500 francs a month towards his housing (though he actually owned his flat) and the family also received 340 francs a month in family allowances. Mme Boursault did not work outside the home; they had three children, aged five, ten and eleven.

M. Leroux, aged 44, was a storekeeper in a firm producing rubber goods. He earned 1,400 francs per month, supplemented by 700 francs family allowance for his four children, aged five, seven, ten and twelve. His wife worked as a concierge, for which she was paid 200 francs a month.

The Boursault apartment, in an older luxury block in the more salubrious part of the *quartier*, comprised 140 square metres (1,400 square feet). There was central heating, a bathroom and lavatory, a fitted kitchen, deep-pile carpeting, a telephone. Mme Leroux's concierge's lodge, where their kitchen was, could not be used for sleeping, being damp and next to a noisy café; the family also rented a room 15 square metres (150 square feet) at the top of the building, on the sixth floor, for which they paid 420 francs a quarter. The room, heated by a coal stove, had a small sink with cold water only. There was no bathroom; the lavatory, on the stairs, was shared with a dozen other families. The family all slept in this room, two of the children sharing one bed.

M. Boursault came from a comfortable background; his father had owned a small business, as had one of his grandfathers; the other grandfather had been an engineer. Mme

Boursault's father was a horticultural engineer and one of her grandfathers an architect. M. Boursault had continued in education until he was 25; he had a science degree. His wife had taken a course in applied art until she was 22; and she had then worked as a publicity assistant until her marriage. The father and grandfather of M. Leroux had been agricultural workers. His wife, an orphan, had been brought up in a Public Assistance institution. The couple had left school at 13 and 14 respectively.

With the children's education, there were no problems for the Boursaults. The two eldest – a boy and a girl – were at private schools, where they were getting on well. The youngest girl was in a public nursery school, but not the nearest – because, in Mme Boursault's words, 'of the kind of children they get there'. All four Leroux children went to the local primary school. The parents did not know what classes they were in, although Mme Leroux said that one was in a special (that is, backward) class.

Most weekends the Boursault family went out of Paris to stay in their second home in the country. M. and Mme Boursault often listened to classical music at home on their stereo set and they sometimes watched films on television; they play bridge regularly. They went to the cinema once a week, to the theatre two or three times a year, to a museum about once a month, and to a restaurant two or three times a week. The main leisure activities of M. and Mme Leroux were watching television and playing with the children. They had been to the cinema only during their holidays, and M. Leroux had in the past occasionally been to watch a football match.

During the year before the interview, Mme Leroux had not been able to go on holiday at all, though her husband had taken the four children away for a month. M. Boursault had been able· to take only five weeks because of his work, but his wife and the three children had been away on holiday for three and half months.

Similar contrasts between privileged and deprived families can obviously be drawn from among the inhabitants of London. In illustrating the Lambeth differences, the names of the two families are again fictitious.

Mr Dawson, an advertising executive earning £6,000 a year, lived with his wife and two children in an eight-roomed Geor-

gian house they were buying on a mortgage. They had engaged
an architect to restore and convert it, putting in two bathrooms
and an open-plan kitchen/dining/day room in the semi-
basement. They had central heating, a washing machine,
dishwasher, fridge and freezer and they were on the telephone.
The front garden was landscaped to take two cars – his Rover
and her Mini. The back garden was part paved, part grassed,
with two mature plane trees; it contained a Wendy house, a
climbing frame and a swing. The youngest child was not yet at
school; the eldest went to a private school about three miles
away. Mr and Mrs Dawson, who had both come from professional class homes, had been to university. They went to the
theatre 'three or four times a year', to concerts with similar
frequency, and to a restaurant for an evening meal about once a
week.

Mr Maddox earned £32 a week as a labourer in a small local
firm producing plastic goods. He had changed jobs five times
during the five years before the interview. He had no formal
qualifications and no training. 'I was never able to learn a
trade; my father died when I was a kid, and I had to go out and
start earning as soon as I could.' He was always seeking a job
with more money, but often found that the new job did not last.
He had been unemployed for three weeks in the previous year.
That, and the £150 they had needed to pay in 'key money' to get
their present home, meant they had few resources. They lived
in two rooms plus a small kitchen, not self-contained, in a
four-storey Victorian house in a grey, treeless, road. They
shared the bathroom and lavatory with three other families;
they had a television set and an old fridge, but no washing
machine, dishwasher, vacuum cleaner or central heating. Mrs
Maddox did not work; there were three children, all aged under
five. The family had no car and consequently had little contact
with relatives or friends; nor were they able easily to take the
children out to a park. Mr Maddox, like his French counter-
part, sometimes went to watch a football match. His wife
seldom went out; they could not afford a baby-sitter and any-
way 'the children wouldn't like it'. Her main leisure activity
was watching television and sewing.

Both the Leroux and Maddox families would have qualified
as being 'in poverty' in terms of the kinds of income measures
used in previous *Poverty Reports*. They were clearly also deprived

in a variety of other ways, and they can therefore be described as cumulatively or multiply so. Their deprivations are of course pointed up by the comparisons with their more fortunate compatriots, who differed from them not only in their current lives but also in education and social background. Thus these examples suggest a familiar conclusion: the influence of social class is at least as powerful in these two places as elsewhere, as shown, for instance, in a recent review of the British data (Central Statistical Office 1975).

The influence of social class

The main index of class used in both studies was the occupation of the so-called 'head of household'. The French 'classes' were as follows: *cadres supérieurs* (senior managers and the like), *cadres moyens*, (junior managers and administrators), *employés* (routine non-manual workers, such as clerks and shop assistants), skilled manual workers, and semi-skilled or unskilled manual workers.

In Paris income was strongly related to occupational class, the average salary among senior managers being about four times that among low-skill manual workers. The routine non-manual workers were the second lowest-paid category, receiving less on average than skilled manual workers. Family allowances and other benefits, and the earnings of other members, contributed to total household income. In general the allowances and benefits contributed more, in absolute terms, to households in the lower-paid categories, but additional earnings worked in the opposite direction; though the proportion of wives working did not differ much from class to class, the wives of higher-paid men were more often themselves in higher-paid jobs.

To get a more accurate overall picture of a household's financial circumstances, its total income needs to be related to household membership. In Folie Mericourt, a simple weighting procedure was adopted, by which the first adult was given a 'weight' of 1.0, second and other adults of 0.7 and children aged 16 or under of 0.5. Household income 'per head' (measured in this way) confirmed the relative poverty of the low-skill manual and routine non-manual workers. About a quarter of each had less than 600 francs a month 'per head', as did just one household of the 43 headed by skilled workers, but none of the managers, senior or junior.

Occupation (and therefore income) was largely determined by people's education or training. Four-fifths of senior managers had left school aged 17 or over; among the semi-skilled and unskilled workers, four-fifths had left at 14 or under. Two-thirds of the senior managers had a degree or the equivalent and most of the rest of them had some other kind of diploma or certificate. Diplomas, and particularly degrees, were much rarer in the other classes.

One can see the same process being repeated when one compares the educational progress of children from different class backgrounds. We have discussed this more fully elsewhere (Aiach and Willmott 1975). The children in Folie Mericourt from the lower social classes were in the worst-equipped and worst-staffed schools, more often behind their peers in their education, more often in 'special' classes, had more often left school early. Their parents were less well informed about education in general or about how their children were doing in particular; they were less in touch with the school, either directly or through parent-teacher associations and the like.

Housing standards also matched social class. Four-fifths of households of semi-skilled and unskilled workers, but none of senior managers, lacked three or four of the range of five housing amenities – WC, bath, hot water, central heating, a separate kitchen. In terms of overcrowding, measured by the number of square metres per household member, one in eight of the senior manager households was 'moderately overcrowded' by official standards (six to ten square metres per person) and none 'severely overcrowded' (five square metres or less per person); but among the households of low-skill workers nearly a third were moderately overcrowded and nearly half severely so, leaving only about a fifth who would be officially defined as at an acceptable French standard.

In the Paris study we combined these and other measures of 'inequality' (covering 28 items altogether) into a cumulative score. The proportions, class by class, who were in the most deprived 25% of households were: senior and junior managers, none; routine non-manual workers, one out of 20; skilled manual workers, just over one in five; semi-skilled and unskilled, over half.

In Lambeth, for reasons already given, less detailed information was collected on deprivation/privilege, and the main
analyses on the subject concentrated on a more limited range
and were handled in different ways. But it is possible to review
briefly the influence of social class in some of the main areas of
life in Lambeth and draw out the similarities and differences
compared with Paris. Analyses were done separately for
households with children so as to make the findings comparable in this respect with those of the Paris study.

Occupations were classified into four 'social classes', based
upon one of the standard official schemes (Office of Population
Censuses and Surveys 1970). These were: professional and
managerial (Social Classes I and II, roughly comparable to the
two French managerial categories), routine non-manual
(Social Class III non-manual, broadly similar to the *employés* in
France), skilled manual (Social Class IV manual), semi-skilled
and unskilled (Social Class IV and V).

Income was of course again related to class. With a somewhat similar procedure to that used in Folie Mericourt, we
calculated the income 'per head' of each household. The
'weightings' given to household members were based on supplementary benefit scales for dependants and, again for consistency with SBC practice, the Lambeth figures were calculated
net of housing costs. The proportions living below the poverty
line used in previous *Poverty Reports* (supplementary benefit
levels plus 20%) were similar in the two non-manual classes – about one in 20 in both; the two manual classes were also
like each other in this respect – about one in five in each were
'in poverty'. In terms of average 'income per head' there was
more of a gradation from class to class: professional and managerial, £18.54; routine non-manual, £16.18; skilled manual,
£15.61; semi-skilled and unskilled, £13.39. Car ownership and
having a telephone reflected both class and income.

The classes differed in the proportions of their members who
were unemployed or who had been off work through unemployment or sickness for three weeks or more during the previous
year: less than one in ten of professional, managerial and
routine non-manual workers, one in seven of skilled manual
workers and over a third of unskilled and semi-skilled. In terms
of other deprivations studied, the differences between the classes were not marked. In housing in particular, measured in

overcrowding and amenities, there were virtually no differences between the social classes in Lambeth.

The method of measuring overall deprivation was, again, different from that used in the Paris study. On the basis of the six selected items, each household was given a deprivation score and a privilege score. In terms of the deprivation score, among the households of professional, managerial and routine non-manual workers alike one in 20 was in the most deprived category (having three or more deprivations out of the possible six) compared with one in six of skilled and one in four of semi-skilled and unskilled. The proportions with privilege scores of three or more were: professional and managerial, two-fifths; routine non-manual, just under a third; skilled, almost one in five; semi-skilled and unskilled, one in seven.

There thus seem to be some differences in the influence of class in the two places. First, it was not related to housing deprivation in Lambeth as it was in Folie Mericourt. Secondly, there is the position of the routine non-manual people in Paris in comparison with what seem like similar non-manual workers in London. In Folie Mericourt the *employés* were almost as deprived as the low-skill manual workers and more so than the skilled. In Lambeth, their counterparts had lives more like those of professional and managerial people than like those of manual workers, skilled or not. This may possibly be partly due to differences in classification in the two countries, but it seems more likely that the families of Paris workers in routine non-manual work really are more deprived, relative to others, than similar sorts of people in inner London.

A further point is about the differences between those at the very 'top' of the social class scale and the rest. In Lambeth, as explained, we combined the two senior categories (Social Classes I and II), although in the Paris study the senior and junior managers had been separately distinguished. This amalgamation was made in Lambeth partly because the sample there included relatively few people in Class I (only 8 of the 300 or so households containing children), but also because, for what the separate figures were worth, they did not suggest that such households were any more 'privileged' than those in Class II.

This, together with what we have already noted about the other non-manual workers, suggests that the spread of class differences may be broader, and the gap between the most privileged and the rest wider, in the Paris district than the London one. This may reflect a difference in the population mix of the two districts, compared with other parts of their cities. Folie Mericourt may contain, along with the poor, more very rich of the kind more common say in Chelsea or parts of Westminster than in the particular area studied in Lambeth. But it also seems likely that the two districts to some extent reflect national differences; there is some evidence that France is a more inegalitarian society than Britain (Mercier 1974).

Immigrants

In Folie Mericourt over a third of the population were immigrants, a higher proportion than in most Paris *quartiers*. Many, both Arab and Jew, had come from former French territories in North Africa – Tunisia, Algeria and Morocco. Others were more recent migrants from Portugal, Spain, Italy and Yugoslavia, who had moved to Paris to do the jobs that Frenchmen are no longer prepared to do. Nine-tenths of immigrant heads of households were manual workers, compared with less than half of the French-born, and half the immigrants were in low-skill jobs compared with less than a fifth of the French-born. Given this close relationship between nationality and occupational status, it follows that much of what we have reported about class differences in Folie Mericourt holds for differences between immigrants and others.

There are, however, several spheres in which the immigrants in Folie Mericourt turned out to be particularly deprived. The most striking example was housing. Immigrants were more often overcrowded; half were 'severely' so compared with one in seven of the French households. They more often had unsatisfactory sleeping arrangements – two children sharing a bed, for instance, or sleeping more than two in a room, or sleeping in a corridor; nearly nine out of ten immigrants had makeshift arrangements of this kind, as against three-fifths of French households.

Immigrants more often lacked the basic amenities mentioned earlier; among immigrant manual workers nearly three-quarters had only one or two out of five, compared with under half of French-born manual workers. The immigrants also paid more for the housing they got; their average rent per square metre was 8.59 francs, as against 5.81 francs for French households.

Although there were some respects in which immigrants in Folie Mericourt were not markedly worse off than other people, their general circumstances, as measured by the overall score, compared unfavourably with those of French families in the same class. Among the manual worker households whose heads were immigrants, half were among the most deprived 25% compared with a fifth of the French households of similar occupational status. In all, three-quarters of the households in the worst-off 25% were immigrants.

The comparison made in Lambeth was not according to whether families were immigrants to Britain but according to the skin colour of the head of household; in the main Lambeth survey this had been chosen as the basis of analysis, since other evidence suggested that (in Britain perhaps more than in France) colour was more crucial an influence than nationality or birthplace.

The first difference between Lambeth and Folie Mericourt was in the relationship between class and colour or nationality. Whereas in Folie Mericourt virtually all immigrant heads of households were of low occupational status, in Lambeth the proportions in the different classes did not vary much by colour. In the Lambeth analyses, as in most of those presented for Folie Mericourt, we held the influence of class constant by comparing the households headed by black and white manual workers.

Blacks in Lambeth were worse off in terms of overcrowding: among manual workers half were living at more than one person per room, compared with a third of whites. Since our measure of overcrowding was one that related the number of people in the household to the number of rooms, it was strongly correlated with the number of children, and this particular finding reflects the larger families among blacks. Almost half of them had three or more children compared with a quarter of white households.

There were no marked differences by colour in the proportions deprived on our various other measures. With income in particular, the proportions 'deprived' were the same among black manual workers as among white. There was, however, a difference at the 'privileged' level end of the income scale. Blacks, in other words, were no more likely to be poor, but they were less likely to be rich.

The pattern was much the same with the cumulative indices of deprivation and privilege. In terms of the general deprivation index, there was no evidence that black manual-worker households were worse off than white. But there was a difference in terms of privilege; one in five white manual-worker households, compared with one in ten black, had a privilege score of three or more out of six.

It is difficult to draw a direct comparison with the Paris study since, as already explained, the sets of indices were different. In particular the Folie Mericourt study used one measure combining deprivation and privilege, whereas that in Lambeth used two separate ones. However, it seems on balance as if, even with class held constant, immigrants in the Paris *quartier* were more at a disadvantage, relative to their neighbours, than were blacks living in Lambeth. The contrast seems especially marked in housing; in Folie Mericourt immigrants were not only more overcrowded than French-born heads of households, as blacks in Lambeth were compared with whites, but they also more often lacked amenities in their homes. In general, they were in the very worst (and, for what they got, the most expensive) housing.

Housing

On both social class and race, the comparisons between the two inner city districts suggest an important conclusion about housing. Households whose heads were of lower occupational status or were immigrants were much worse housed than other people in Folie Mericourt, but not in Lambeth.

The Lambeth study was, like Folie Mericourt, in only one area and the conclusions must be interpreted cautiously. But it looks as if the Lambeth research calls into question one of the stock ideas about the so-called 'cycle of deprivation'. In the characteristic diagrams portraying this cycle, the assumption is made that low income usually goes with bad housing (South East Joint Planning Team 1971, SNAP 1972). After studying not just households with children but ·a general sample of households, the Lambeth preliminary report on multiple deprivation, already mentioned, concluded that 'low income and bad housing are not all that strongly associated with each other' (Department of the Environment 1975a). The same conclusion had been suggested by Lucy Syson and Michael Young, reporting their Bethnal Green poverty survey in *Poverty Report 1974:* 'Very few of the income poor were particularly badly off for housing' (Syson and Young 1974). What is true in this respect of Bethnal Green and part of Lambeth is, clearly, not true of the Paris *quartier*.

The point is underlined by a direct comparison of income and housing in Lambeth and Folie Mericourt. In both places, households were divided into three categories depending on the level of 'income per head' (measured in the ways described earlier): a rich minority, a poor minority and a majority falling between the two extremes. The way in which households in these income categories varied in housing in the two places is show in Table 10.1. Since the income levels and the indices of overcrowding and amenities are not the same in both districts, too much must not be made of the detailed comparisons between them, but the measures roughly correspond to each other and are therefore some sort of broad guide.

Table 10.1   Income per head and housing in Folie Mericourt and Lambeth
(Households containing at least one child aged 16 or under)

	Overcrowding	*'Rich'*	*'Majority'*	*'Poor'*	*All*
Folie	% ten sq. metres or less				
Mericourt	per person	0%	71%	89%	63%
	Total number	17	93	19	129
Lambeth	% more than one person				
	per room	0%	39%	31%	35%
	Total number (weighted)	19	221	71	311
	Amenities				
Folie	% none or one (of five)	0%	57%	83%	74%
Mericourt	Total number	16	83	18	117
Lambeth	% three or less (of seven)	5%	11%	7%	10%
	Total number (weighted)	19	221	71	311

The total numbers in Folie Mericourt vary, and add up to less than the full sample of 138 households, because on some items adequate information was not available for some households. Some households in Lambeth have had to be excluded for the same reason. The Lambeth totals are described as 'weighted' because, as in all the analyses, a re-weighting procedure was used to compensate for the deliberate under-representation in the original sample of households living on local authority estates (the procedure is explained in Department of the Environment 1974b)

The first point about Table 10.1 is that it confirms the general impression stated earlier about the two places. In both, the rich are clearly well off for housing; none or very few 'rich' households were overcrowded or without basic amenities. The crucial comparison is that between the 'poor' households and the majority. In Lambeth those poor in income were neither more overcrowded nor worse off for amenities; in Folie Mericourt they were. Thus the association between low income and bad housing had been broken in Lambeth as it had not in the Paris *quartier*.

It does not follow that Lambeth is typical of London, still less of all Britain. Last year's Camden survey found that there 'the connection between poverty and bad housing had not been removed' (Syson and Young 1975). Further analyses have been made both of the Camden survey and of data from a social survey carried out in connection with another inner area study, also funded by the Department of the Environment, in Small Heath, Birmingham (see Department of the Environment 1975b). These analyses, of overcrowding and housing amenities in terms of income per head, social class and colour, present a less clear-cut picture than in Lambeth; in both places there is evidence of some association between these other characteristics and bad housing.

The explanation for these variations between British inner city districts lies in their different proportions of council housing. In Lambeth nearly half the households were council tenants, in Camden a third and in Small Heath just under a quarter. It is clear that in Lambeth the reason why not only low-skill households but also black households are not markedly deprived in housing is that they have access to the local authority stock. It is true that blacks are more often in the older and less desirable property (Department of the Environment 1974b), and therefore that in terms of a more refined analysis of housing quality they might well be judged relatively worse off than others, but the general point remains valid. In the Lambeth study area, if not in other districts, blacks have managed to join low-skill whites in surmounting the barriers to council housing, and in consequence a vital link in the 'cycle of deprivation' has been weakened.

If the presence of council housing is the key to the Lambeth findings, its absence seems as crucial in Folie Mericourt. The

French equivalent to council housing is the 'social housing' provided by cooperative bodies such as the *Habitation à Loyer Modéré* (HLM). In Folie Mericourt, as far as we can tell, there is no HLM housing at all; certainly none was built in the 15 years up to 1969. In the *arrondissement* of which Folie Mericourt is part – the 11th – 900 HLM dwellings were built over the 15-year period, compared with 8,000 new private dwellings.

It has been very different in Lambeth. In the area of study the number of council dwellings increased by nearly 2,000 between 1961 and 1971, while virtually no new private housing was built and the total number of private dwellings fell. In inner London as a whole, 31% of households were council tenants by 1971. In outer London the proportion was lower – 21%.

In the Paris region the majority of HLM homes have been built in giant high-rise estates in the suburbs, while inside Paris (roughly comparable in population size to inner London) the main emphasis has been on building private luxury apartments. In 1973, only 8% of all the housing inside Paris was HLM, compared with 23% in the rest of the region.

It could be argued that, for Parisians, the location of HLM housing matters less than its availability. But there are a number of obstacles in the way of many of the poor families of Folie Mericourt, even if they felt able and willing to move to the suburbs. One difficulty is that an HLM apartment is not available to those with low incomes. An earlier French Minister of Housing estimated that 20% of families in the Paris region were ineligible on this score (*Le Monde* 13 November 1969); the proportion would clearly be much higher in a district like Folie Mericourt. A second problem, which particularly affects the immigrants, is that there is a quota: the proportion of 'priority' allocations which can go to immigrants is limited to 17%.

Without council housing or its equivalent, people in Folie Mericourt could be helped if there were an effective system to subsidise their housing costs. The French government has had a system of housing allowances since 1948 (see Lawson and Stevens 1974). Again, however, most poor familes in our sample were not benefiting; this was because the payment of allowances was conditional on the dwelling being in good physical condition, having certain standard amenities and not being overcrowded.

The conclusion we draw is that, apart from other points of comparison between the Paris and London districts, the contrast in housing illustrates the potential role that public intervention can play in reducing deprivation. We would not want it to be thought that the comparison we make is intended to be any kind of final judgement on the housing policies of France and Britain, or of Paris and London. For one thing, there are the limitations in the studies that we have already pointed out. There were two districts only and, if Folie Mericourt was selected because its housing was specially bad, the Lambeth district was relatively well-endowed with council dwellings. Furthermore, French policies are currently changing; the system of housing allowances in particular is being altered in an attempt to direct more help to the poor and the badly housed. But we think that the interim conclusions we have drawn remain valid – as findings that would probably hold up in a broader and more rigorously comparative study of deprivation in inner London and inner Paris, and also as pointers to the kind of perspectives that can be gained from comparative research.

References

P. Aiach (1975) *Vivre à Folie Mericourt: Étude des Processus Cumulatifs d'Inégalités*, Institut National de la Santé et de la Recherche Médicale, France

P. Aiach and P. Willmott (1975) 'Inequality and education in the East End of Paris', *New Society*, 9 October 1975

Central Statistical Office (1975) 'Social commentary; social class', *Social Trends* no. 6, HMSO

Department of the Environment (1974a) *Lambeth Inner Area Study: Project Report* (IAS/LA/1)

Department of the Environment (1974b) *Lambeth Inner Area Study: People, Housing and District* (IAS/LA/5)

Department of the Environment (1975a) *Lambeth Inner Area Study: Poverty and Multiple Deprivation* (IAS/LA/10)

Department of the Environment (1975b) *Birmingham Inner Area Study: A Social Survey* (IAS/B/5)

R. Lawson and C. Stevens (1974) 'Housing allowances in West Germany and France', *Journal of Social Policy*, vol. 3, Part 3

P-A. Mercier (1974) *Les inégalités en France*, CREDOC, France

Office of Population Censuses and Surveys (1970) *Classification of Occupations*, HMSO

South East Joint Planning Team (1971) *Strategic Plan for the South East. Studies vol. 2. Social and Environmental Aspects*, HMSO

SNAP (1972) *Another Chance for Cities*, Liverpool Shelter Neighbourhood Action Project (Sponsored by Shelter)

L. Syson and M. Young (1974) 'Poverty in Bethnal Green', M. Young (ed.) *Poverty Report 1974*, Temple Smith

L. Syson and M. Young (1975) 'The Camden Survey', M. Young (ed.) *Poverty Report 1975*, Temple Smith

Research on poverty can help to deepen understanding and suggest lessons for policy. This review of recent and current studies shows something of what has been done. It also shows how much remains to be done.

11 Recent research on income poverty in Britain

LUCY SYSON

Britain has a long tradition of survey research into poverty, going back to the pioneering work of Charles Booth and Seebohm Rowntree (Jones 1949). Interest in the subject waned from the mid 1930s until the late 1950s, but then began to revive, and since the early 1960s there has been a resurgence of poverty research; much of the work done in that period has been recently reviewed by Sinfield (1975).

The aim of this chapter is to concentrate on research done more recently – over the last five years or so – and on some still in progress. The main purpose is to review and assess the work, while at the same time drawing attention to some of the findings.

I have to start with two caveats. First, although I have tried to be reasonably comprehensive, it is impossible to be exhaustive in a review of this kind, and some relevant studies may have been excluded. Secondly, as the title implies, the chapter is concerned with poverty only in terms of current income. This is not, of course, because income poverty should be seen as the only, or necessarily the most important kind. The whole debate about 'deprivation' has shown that even if the exact meaning of the word is difficult to pin down, the lack of money is often the result or cause of other problems faced by the same household. But if the rediscovery of 'poverty' after the complacent 1950s is fairly recent, the introduction of the broader concept of 'deprivation' and the efforts to define it are even more so. It would in any case take a whole book to cover research into all the various aspects of potential deprivation – housing, education and so on. Research on 'deprivation' is therefore mentioned here only when the particular study includes some examination of income poverty, as for example some Inner Area Studies (IAS) and Community Development Projects (CDP).

Methods of research

Various methods can be used in studying poverty. So far, apart from the unpublished inquiry in 1968 (Townsend forthcoming), there has been no national survey on the subject. What has been done instead is to use national data collected for other purposes but whose sample has contained enough low-income families to allow some special analyses. The annual Family Expenditure Survey has been the main source of this kind.

A second type of research is the kind of theoretical exercise which examines, for example, how new levels of taxation or means-tested benefits would affect 'standard' families of different size with different incomes. This work is categorised here as 'theoretical' in that either no original data are used (eg Nevitt 1972 and forthcoming) or, if they are, the statistical exercises performed on them are more relevant to the results than the original data themselves (McClements 1975).

A third method is the collection of original data, either in sample surveys by use of questionnaires or in more intensive interviews with people in a particular category, such as the unemployed or the disabled – intensive studies of this kind, though not statistically representative, can throw important light on the problems people face. Survey research can be national or local. The common feature is that individual people and families can be and are described through formal or informal face-to-face interviews.

The three-fold distinction – secondary analysis of national data, 'theoretical' studies and survey research – is used as the basis of the discussion that follows.

The use of secondary data

Several national surveys collect data about a large number of individuals and households each year or at regular intervals. A study of the income analysis in their published reports provides an accessible summary of the differing fortunes of different income and other special groups in this country. For example, the Family Expenditure Survey (FES) (Department of Employment 1974a) includes tables for pensioner and single-parent households, the General Household Survey (GHS) has made some preliminary analysis to show the incomes of 'income units' (Office of Population Censuses and Surveys 1975); the National Food Survey (NFS) shows what happens in families of different size with different gross incomes (Ministry of Agriculture 1974); and the New Earnings Survey (NES) helps to identify low-paid workers (results published in Department of Employment *Gazette*), as do other regular inquiries by the Department of Employment (see for example, the DE *Gazette* every February for the results of the annual October inquiry into earnings of manual workers). Other sources of information are the Census and the Inland Revenue figures (Board of Inland Revenue 1973), although the latter have the important limitation that they deal only with tax-payers.

The difficulty with all this information is that, in the form in which it is published, low-income households are not identified in any consistent way (that is, allowing for household size, ages of children and so on) and in any case the number of such households in the national surveys are relatively few – too few for much cross-analysis. The 1971 Census was followed up by a postal income inquiry into 1% of households. Unfortunately the response was low (55%) and no results were available at the time of writing. It is therefore not possible to say how useful this will be in identifying low-income households which might be analysed in terms of other household characteristics.

The difficulty remains, therefore, that there are no published data from the surveys mentioned above which describe the 'poor'. Until a method is devised for drawing a sample which over-represents the kind of people likely to be poor, a national survey of the poor will continue to be expensive. As Abel-Smith and Townsend stated in *The Poor and the Poorest* (1965):

> Rather than seek immediately to launch a time-consuming and expensive survey we felt that every effort should first be made to explore existing information.

Their re-analysis of the 1953-54 and 1960 Ministry of Labour family expenditure inquiries was able to take account of the structure of individual households, to measure their net disposable income (either as actual income or as shown by the expenditure pattern) and to judge how many were poor compared with the basic national assistance scales. Several precedents were set by this research: the use of Family Expenditure Survey data for measuring the extent of poverty, the use of the national assistance (later supplementary benefit) scales as the criteria of poverty and, most important of all, a revival of interest in the whole question of how much poverty existed in Britain.

Several studies using FES data are now in progress. The National Institute of Economic and Social Research is engaged in a general study of low-income households using the 1971 FES data. This includes a study of the needs of children of different ages (Hansard 8 July 1975) as well as an examination of the unit of analysis best suited to a discussion of poverty – should it be a household's income units or simply individuals? (Fiegehen and Lansley 1975).

At the Centre for Studies in Social Policy, Barnes is analysing past FES data; although the surveys were started before 1967, he is using that date as the starting one for most of his analyses because in that year the national sample was doubled. The full results of this study will, it is hoped, be published in 1976.

Both these and the Abel-Smith/Townsend studies were fairly general studies of the poor, taken from rather different angles and using different methods of analysis. The Department of Health and Social Security (DHSS) has done some more specialised studies of its own, notably that on two-parent families (Howe 1971) where the concept of 'net disposable resources' was used. Income net of tax, national insurance and housing costs and taking account of family structure was, as in *The Poor and the Poorest*, measured against theoretical supplementary benefit entitlement.

The DHSS now routinely analyses FES data by income unit (or 'family', as it is sometimes described), occupational status of head of household, whether receiving supplementary benefit and, if not, how the net disposable income relates to theoretical entitlement. Figures for 1973 are given in *Social Trends No. 6* (Central Statistical Office 1975) and a figure for 1974, supplied by the DHSS, is included in Table 11.1 later in this chapter.

'Theoretical' research
Several studies under this heading use data from the national surveys already mentioned. For example, recent developments

in national policies trying to deal with poverty and deprivation seem to have been based on the assumption that specific areas can be located where most or many of the problems exist and where a reasonably high proportion of all the people have some or all of the problems thought of as 'deprivation' including, by implication, low incomes. This assumption has now been tested in several ways.

In connection with the Urban Deprivation Unit's work at the Home Office, the Department of the Environment has completed a series of analyses of 1971 Census data at enumeration district level. The aim of these analyses was to see how wide were the variations between the amounts of 'deprivation' (overcrowding, for example, or proportion of pensioner households) in different enumeration districts (EDs) and whether the 'worst' EDs that is, with the highest proportion of each 'deprivation') overlapped for different indicators; also what proportion of all households suffering a particular deprivation were to be found in the 'worst' EDs.

No direct information on incomes could, of course, be included, since this is not contained in the 100% or 10% census samples, and no attempt was made to use other census indicators as proxies for income. There was no evidence available to show what indicator or combination of indicators might be the best. But it is worth mentioning this work, since the results show that, except for Clydeside, the geographical overlap between the chosen indicators (most of which had an *a priori* connection with poverty or deprivation) was less than would have been expected and that only a minority of the people suffering each deprivation lived in the 'worst' areas (that is, the enumeration districts where that deprivation was concentrated) (Department of the Environment 1974-75).

Two rather more direct attempts to find the links between income and census data are in progress. One, by Rothman, is using General Household Survey income data, analysing it on a ward basis (Office of Population Censuses and Surveys 1975). The aim is to produce an 'income surrogate' so as to be able to predict the average income of small areas or individual households from other known facts about them. The other study is a small one being carried out at the Institute of Community Studies. Here the geographical base is the enumeration district and the income data (average net disposable income per head) are drawn from the Institute's Camden survey described in

Poverty Report 1975.

Other research is concerned with income allowances for children. As Bagley (1969) has pointed out, there seems to be neither consistency nor any clear rationale in how children are treated according to what benefit their parents receive. For some benefits (national insurance allowances and family allowances) the important question is how many children there are in the family. For taxation, the amount of benefit depends partly on the actual income of the family (if the income is too low then the family receives no benefit at all from child allowances) and partly on the age of the child. For many means-tested benefits, there is a standard allowance for each child. For supplementary benefits the scales are graded according to the age of the child alone.

Since it is clearly impossible for all the allowances to be 'correct', this is an important area for research. It is relevant to the study of poverty because, apart from tax allowances and family allowances, the benefits concerned and any changes in their levels most affect low-income families. The main study in this field is being carried out by the Department of Health and Social Security, using data from the 1971 and 1972 Family Expenditure Surveys (McClements 1975). The work at the DHSS is being complemented by a similar exercise as part of the National Institute of Economic and Social Research's broader project on low incomes, mentioned earlier.

There are two continuous exercises on the effects of different tax and benefit rates on families of different structure with different incomes. One is by the Department of Health and Social Security, the other a collaborative study by Nevitt at the London School of Economics, Roberti of the Centre for Studies in Social Policy and Bradshaw of York University. While the DHSS exercise is described as 'the use of a computer to simulate the interaction of changes in earnings, taxation and entitlement to means-tested benefits, using Family Expenditure Survey data, to produce estimates of the numbers of families entitled to means-tested benefits and those subject to high marginal rates of tax' (Hansard 8 July 1975), the second project's aim is to identify those people who would really benefit from cash transfers involved in national redistributive policies.

The aims are not perhaps very different. An example of the DHSS work was included in *Social Trends No. 5* (Central Statistical Office 1974) where the 'poverty trap' was illustrated, showing how an increase of one pound in gross income would be eaten away in lost benefits and increased tax liability.

Other studies focus on the major theme of this book as a whole – the effects of inflation on people with low incomes. In addition to the analyses in *Poverty Reports,* the work includes a survey of 60 poor families by the Child Poverty Action Group (Brown and Field 1974) and a collection of papers concerning the old, the disabled and the low paid published by the Fabian Society (1975). Attitudes towards inflation were tested by PEP and reported in July 1975 (Daniel 1975).

Special surveys

As already mentioned, one national survey of poverty has so far been undertaken, in 1967-68. Unfortunately the results are not yet available (but see Townsend forthcoming). However, other studies have been carried out which if not statistically 'national', were at least geographically widespread.

The unemployed seem to have been particularly thoroughly covered. For example, the Department of Employment carried out in June 1973 (Department of Employment 1974b) a survey on the characteristics of the unemployed which provides useful basic material. As part of a large DHSS-sponsored study, some detailed research about the chronically and frequently unemployed, including information about incomes, has already been reported (Hill *et al* 1973). Daniels, for PEP, has reported on a national survey of 1,479 unemployed people interviewed in October 1973 (Daniels 1974).

The specific aim of *Workless* by Marsden and Duff (1975) was to fill the gaps left by large-scale sample surveys, useful though these are for providing the statistical background. Interviews were carried out in 1971 in south-east and north-east England with about 60 families, using tape recorders and, with some, a camera. The core of the book is the actual words of the unemployed, describing their attitudes to work, their attempts to find new jobs, their difficulties in managing their income, their problems of debt and changes in family relationships.

As for old and retired people, Age Concern sometimes reviews their circumstances (e.g. Hewitt 1974) and it has commissioned research about attitudes among the general public towards the level of pensions (Age Concern 1974). Some questions have been added to the General Household Survey concerning knowledge of payment procedures among pensioners.

The Department of Health and Social Security has carried out several surveys of families in particular categories. One study, of 348 families receiving supplementary benefit, compared the circumstances of fatherless families and of families whose heads were long-term sick and unemployed (Marshall 1972). In a more recent DHSS study, 614 recipients of Family Income Supplement were interviewed (Knight and Nixon 1975). Families with two or more children were interviewed as part of a national survey in June 1966 (Ministry of Social Security 1967).

About the same time a small supplementary study was carried out in London (Land 1969). The latter concentrated on families with five or more dependent children and a good deal of information was collected both about income and the more important kinds of expenditure. Although the survey covered families over a broad income range, the circumstances of those at the lower end were particularly stressed in the report, which was a pilot study for the national poverty survey by Townsend.

The Child Poverty Action Group carried out a study of families with three or more children (Bottomley 1971) but the sample there neither was, nor was claimed to be, representative of large families as a class. Only 14 families completed an expenditure diary and took part in the follow-up interview. The results are useful rather in the same way as *Workless*, throwing light on the individual problems faced by these families rather than as generalisations about all such families.

For two other important and sometimes overlapping groups, the statistical probability is that many will be poor. These are the sick and disabled on the one hand and single-parent families on the other. Major official studies have been carried out on both groups. For the disabled, there is the study carried out by the Office of Population Censuses and Surveys (OPCS) in 1968-69 (Harris *et al* 1972) which not only tried to define carefully the standards by which different degrees of impairment could be measured (for example, ability to cut one's own toe nails or go to the lavatory alone) but also the problems and characteristics, including income, of the disabled and their families. An important finding was that just over 7% of the sample of 12,738 were entitled to but not receiving supplementary benefit and that 30% were already receiving it.

One-parent families have been the subject of a recent official national survey as well as investigation by a special committee which collected much additional evidence. The two reports which resulted (Hunt *et al* 1973; Finer 1974) brought together an immense amount of information about one-parent families, while the evidence submitted to the committee, for example by the National Council for One-Parent Families, provided even more. The Hunt survey was carried out in five areas with a sample of about 2,000 households in each, where comparisons between one-parent and two-parent families were made on many aspects of life, including income. Because the interviewers were instructed to proceed with some questions only if the household income was below a certain level, a fairly simple measure was taken rather than calculating theoretical entitlement to supplementary benefit.

Three other studies on one-parent families help to illustrate the figures. The most comprehensive, based on 116 interviews with some mothers on national assistance in 1965 and 1966 (Marsden 1973) was specifically concerned with poverty. Another, by the National Council for One-Parent Families, was a report on the first hundred letters received by their office in response to a request in 33 local newspapers for information about child-minding problems (Blake 1972). 85 out of the 100 mentioned poverty as one of their main problems. Loneliness was also frequently mentioned. The most recent study, by the Child Poverty Action Group (Streather and Weir 1974), looked at 40 cases of people who had come to their Citizens' Rights Office. Those selected for study were all on social security, but this was clearly a somewhat biased sample, like those who had felt strong, articulate or bitter enough to write to the National Council for One-Parent Families.

Local poverty studies

In local research, as at the national level, few surveys have been designed to find out the characteristics of 'the poor', however defined. Nevertheless, the results of several studies bear closely on the level of poverty in any one area – for example, surveys of the take-up of means-tested benefits or of particular groups of people in the area.

The straightforward local poverty research can be divided into two kinds. One is the 'snap-shot' type, that is, a once-only survey describing poverty at one particular moment. The second is the longitudinal type, where the same people or their descendants are interviewed at different times in order to see what changes have taken place.

The earliest of the more recent 'snap-shot' surveys (the term is intended to be descriptive, not derogatory) was that carried out in the St Ann's district of Nottingham in 1966 (Coates and Silburn 1967 and 1970). The authors did not suggest that their sample was representative of the whole of the city of Nottingham. But they did think that it could be typical of other 'twilight urban areas' and it is worth quoting their main findings in that context. These are compared with those for other local surveys, and with a national calculation based on Family Expenditure Survey data, in Table 11.1.

Table 11.1   Proportion of families living below 120% of supplementary benefit entitlement in selected areas

Area	Date	% below 120% SB[1]	Total number of families in sample	Source
St Ann's	1966	26	176	Coates and Silburn 1967
Bethnal Green	1973	31	243	*Poverty Report 1974*
Lambeth (part)	1973	24	728	Department of the Environment forthcoming
Small Heath	1974	17	737	Department of the Environment forthcoming
Camden	1974	18	525	*Poverty Report 1975*
Great Britain[2]	1974	19	8307	Department of Health and Social Security (figures supplied)

1   SB= supplementary benefit (formerly national assistance). The choice of 120% of basic entitlement as a suitable poverty line is explained in Syson and Young (1974).

2   Based on Family Expenditure Survey data.

Two other local surveys are those described in the first two *Poverty Reports* (Syson and Young 1974 and 1975). The first was a small pilot study in Bethnal Green in 1973. In a small follow-up study in 1974 people were re-interviewed and the results analysed to see who was still poor, who had slipped into poverty in the interim and who had managed to move above the poverty line. The data were also used to calculate the effects of inflation on the sample as a whole, using different retail price indices for different types of household, as recommended by Trinder (1975). The 1974 sample was no longer, of course, a random one, partly because of a rather high refusal rate in the first year, mainly because only 161 out of the original 243 could both be traced and persuaded to cooperate a second time so soon after the first. Enough people were seen, though, for it to be clear that there was a hard core majority in long-term poverty plus a minority who did change their status from one year to the next (Jones and Young 1975).

The other poverty survey carried out by the Institute of Cmmunity Studies, in the London Borough of Camden, was also in its way a pilot study. This was a study in a relatively 'mixed' area, which made it possible both to test in a limited way the extent of geographical concentration of poverty in small areas, and, as referred to earlier, to see how, if at all, the information collected about household incomes in 1974 could be related to much other information collected for the same area (but not necessarily the same people) in the Census of 1971. The extent to which such a connection existed at the level of polling districts is discussed in a document presented to the DHSS (Syson 1975) and the data are now being re-analysed by computer for enumeration districts.

Another smaller study was carried out in 1971 in York by Maynard (1972). There, 30 families in two selected 'low income' areas were interviewed, the choice of family being left to the interviewer. This again can be regarded more as a pilot study (which indeed was what it was intended to be), plus a series of case studies of individual families, than as an attempt to measure the extent or nature of poverty in York or even a part of the city. In 1974 an effort was made to re-interview the original families but only 12 of the 1971 sample were contacted.

No longitudinal studies have yet been reported on. Data are clearly needed to inform the debate about 'the life cycle of deprivation' (that is the level of poverty encountered at different stages of one person's lifetime) and that about 'transmitted deprivation' (the question of whether poverty is somehow pas-

sed on from one generation to the next). In their evidence to the
Royal Commission on the Distribution of Income and Wealth,
Atkinson and Trinder (1975) made the case for much better
knowledge in this area. They are themselves interviewing the
sons and daughters of the people seen in York in 1950
(Rowntree and Lavers 1951).

Another longitudinal study forms part of a proposal by the
North Tyneside Community Development Project to examine
the impact of income maintenance services (North Tyneside
CDP 1975); the intention is to re-interview as many as possible
of the sample of 92 unemployed first visited by Sinfield in'
1963-64 (Sinfield 1970). At the time of the original survey, 89 of
the 92 had incomes below 140% of supplementary benefit scale
rates and half the families with children had incomes below
even their basic entitlement (largely because of the 'wage stop',
now abolished). Sinfield is the research consultant for the
repeat survey, so there is certainty of continuity for this particular project.

Although the number of surveys specifically dealing with the
extent and nature of poverty in different areas is few, a certain
amount of relevant local information is available. For example,
the National Community Development Project (1974) has
shown that of the twelve areas at least four – in Coventry,
Batley, Birmingham and Paisley – were carrying out research
related to income and especially the take-up of means-tested
benefits. Some reports on this work are available, for example
on the use of local official data such as the number of households receiving free school meals or family income supplement,
together with the number of families with rent arrears (Mackay
1974).

In another government-sponsored programme, the Inner
Area Studies, information has been collected by means of
household surveys which included questions on income in part
of the London Borough of Lambeth and in Small Heath, Birmingham (see Table 11.1). Analysis, directed by Willmott, of
these data together with those from the Camden survey already
mentioned, is proceeding at the Institute of Community
Studies as part of the work on multiple deprivation described in
the previous chapter (see Department of the Environment 1975
and forthcoming).

Two large surveys by the Greater London Council contained

questions on income which could prove useful in an analysis of income distribution. One was a survey carried out in 1967 (Greater London Council 1970) in connection with housing conditions in London. The aim was to try to trace families where there was a housing need (such as young married couples living with parents) not identifiable from a simple census count of households. Over 7,000 addresses were in the stratified and clustered sample, and several analyses based on income were produced, though not in a form comparable with any of the poverty surveys mentioned earlier.

The second, even bigger, survey was the 1971 Greater London Transportation Survey when nearly 50,000 households were interviewed. Unfortunately 15% of those interviewed failed to give information about income, so some interpolation of results was necessary. Not much has been published about this aspect of the survey but an analysis of the geographical distribution of incomes to see whether poverty is concentrated in the inner zone has been made (Berthoud forthcoming). Gross household income was the financial basis of the analysis, electoral wards the geographical one. After examining variations between and within wards and between and within 'inner' and 'outer' London, Berthoud concluded that poverty is 'apparently more common in the inner areas, but it is neither general in the inner rings, nor absent from the outer rings'. He found housing tenure a good predictor of average ward incomes, together with membership of 'inner' or 'outer' ring.

Mention has already been made of research on take-up; the topic was included, for example, in the Camden and Bethnal Green poverty studies. There are other surveys where this is the main focus. A major one, still being analysed at the time of writing, is that by the Department of the Environment in Haringey. The focus of this has been the effect of seven different types of publicity on take-up of rent allowances in similar areas of the borough. The disappointing but perhaps not surprising result was that even after an intensive exercise which included, at the end, 'blanket' publicity over the whole borough, only 25% of eligible tenants were receiving rent allowances and 20% of all the tenants interviewed 'hadn't heard' of them (Lewis 1975). The most successful – and cheapest – form of publicity turned out to be direct mailing of the government leaflet.

The Child Poverty Action Group, together with its local branches, has organised a number of small surveys on this subject and one fairly large one. The latter, on rate rebates, was in Islington in 1971 and the report now forms part of the basic literature on means tests (Meacher 1972). Other local branches of the Child Poverty Action Group have between them covered educational benefits, family allowances, Family Income Supplement and rent allowances (York Child Poverty Action Group 1974; Tunbridge Wells Child Poverty Action Group 1974 and 1975; Preston Child Poverty Action Group 1972a and 1972b), mostly with quite small samples but illustrating a little of the geographical variation that must be common.

Conclusions
Although there remain problems, for example about how to ensure that one collects reliable information about income, who should be interviewed and what should be taken as the 'poverty line', it is clear that much useful research has been done or is in train. Techniques have improved, particularly in the use of computers to explore relationships between income poverty and other things. But it is also clear that there are some important gaps.

One is about the differences between the economic behaviour of the poor and the non-poor. For example, do the poor pay more for the same goods and services because they are not able to travel far or buy in large quantities? (Piachaud 1974). This question, as well as the related one of whether non-working housewives receive enough housekeeping allowance to keep them and their children out of poverty, is a concern of the National Consumer Council, which sponsored some modest research (on housekeeping allowances, on shop prices, on the interest rates of different forms of credit and on paying for gas and electricity) for its first conference in September 1975 (National Consumer Council 1975). The Council intends to pursue this line of inquiry.

Another area where knowledge about poverty is sparse concerns people living in institutions, and the homeless. Even if there have been a few separate studies and reports such as that by the Grassmarket Urban Aid Project on homeless single people in Edinburgh and their welfare rights (Rooney and Woolf 1975), no attempt seems to have been made to bring together the results of that kind of research with that on domestic households (which are all that are reported on in the official surveys such as the Family Expenditure Survey and the General Household Survey, frequently quoted in this chapter).

The biggest gap in poverty research is the absence of a regular national poverty survey. Of course, local studies and other specialised research of the kinds discussed in this chapter can make a useful contribution to understanding some of the causes and consequences of poverty. But such studies need to be complemented by the kind of nationwide research that alone can provide the essential information about the extent of poverty and the characteristics of the poor.

There is currently a good deal of interest in the possibility of national poverty research, both inside and outside government circles. The major difficulty is that of sampling. What is needed is a method which will allow one to avoid too large – and thus too expensive – a sample; to do this one needs to 'over-sample' poor people and in such a way that the results can be validly re-weighted to produce a sample representing the whole population. The case for cross-national surveys of poverty was put by Michael Young in *Poverty Report 1975* and is echoed by Peter Willmott and Pierre Aiach in the preceding chapter. But, quite apart from the cross-national advantages, we clearly need national studies to provide national governments with reliable evidence about the composition and circumstances of the poor, and about variations between regions, between town and country and between inner and outer urban zones.

Already, as Table 11.1 shows, we know something about the extent of poverty, nationally and in some selected districts (using the now widely accepted 'poverty line' of supplementary benefits plus 20%). The need now is, while advancing in other kinds of research as well, to move to a more securely based discussion about who the poor are, where they live and how their needs could be more effectively met.

References

B. Abel-Smith and P. Townsend (1965) *The Poor and the Poorest, London School of Economics Occasional Papers on Social Administration* no. 17, Bell
Age Concern (1974) *Public Opinion on Pensions*
A.B. Atkinson and C. Trinder (January 1975) *Intergenerational Income Mobility,*

·evidence to the Royal Commission on the Distribution of Income and Wealth

C. Bagley (1969) *The Cost of a Child: Problems in the Relief and Measurement of Poverty*, Institute of Psychiatry

R. Berthoud (forthcoming) *Where Are London's Poor?*

P. Blake (1972) *The Plight of One-Parent Families*, Council for Children's Welfare

Board of Inland Revenue (1973) *The Survey of Personal Incomes 1970-71*, HMSO

V. Bottomley (1971) *Families with Low Incomes in London*, Poverty pamphlet 8, Child Poverty Action Group

M. Brown and F. Field (1974) *Poor Families and Inflation*, Child Poverty Action Group

Central Statistical Office (1974) *Social Trends no. 5*, HMSO

Central Statistical Office (1975) *Social Trends no. 6*, HMSO

K. Coates and R. Silburn (1967) *St Ann's: Poverty, Deprivation and Morale in a Nottingham Community*, Nottingham University

K. Coates and R. Silburn (1970) *Poverty, the Forgotten Englishman*, Penguin

W.W. Daniel (1974) *A National Survey of the Unemployed*, PEP Broadsheet no. 546

W.W. Daniel (1975) *The PEP Survey on inflation*, PEP Broadsheet no. 553

Department of Employment (1974a) *Family Expenditure Survey: report for 1973*, HMSO

Department of Employment (1974b) 'Characteristics of the unemployed: sample survey June 1973', *Department of Employment Gazette*, March 1974, HMSO

Department of the Environment (1974-75) *Census Indicators of Urban Deprivation, working notes*

Department of the Environment (1975) *Lambeth Inner Area Study: Poverty and Multiple Deprivation* (IAS/LA/10)

Department of the Environment (forthcoming) *Lambeth Inner Area Study: Second Report on Multiple Deprivation*

Fabian Society (1975) *Inflation and Low Incomes*, Fabian Research Series 322 (see also under P. Lewis, C. Pond, P. Townsend and A. Walker)

G. Fiegehen and P.A. Lansley (1975) *A Note on Household Size and Income Unit in the Measurement of Poverty*, paper presented to the 14th General Conference of the International Association for Research in Income and Wealth, Aulanko, Finland

Finer Report (1974) *Report of the Committee on One-Parent Families*, HMSO

Greater London Council (1970) *The Characteristics of London's Households*, Research Report no. 5

A. Harris, C. Smith and E. Head (1972) *Income and Entitlement to Supplementary Benefit of Impaired People in Great Britain*, Part III of *Handicapped and Impaired in Great Britain*, HMSO

P. Hewitt (1974) *Age Concern on Pensioner Incomes*, Age Concern

M.J. Hill, R.M. Harrison and A.V. Sergeant (1973) *Men Out of Work*, Cambridge University Press

J.R. Howe (1971) *Two-Parent Families: a Study of their Resources and Needs*, DHSS statistical series no. 14, HMSO

A. Hunt, J. Fox and M. Morgan (1973) *Families and their Needs*, HMSO

D. Caradog Jones (1949) *Social Surveys,* Hutchinson

I. Jones and M. Young (1975) 'The repeat survey in Bethnal Green', M. Young (ed) *Poverty Report 1975,* Temple Smith

I.B. Knight and J.M. Nixon (1975) *Two-Parent Families in Receipt of Family Income Supplement,* DHSS Statistical and Research Report Series, No. 9, HMSO

H. Land (1969) *Large Families in London,* London School of Economics, *Occasional Papers on Social Administration* no. 32, Bell

P. Lewis (1975) 'Pensions, savings and inflation', *Inflation and Low Incomes,* Fabian Research Series 322, Fabian Society

T. Lewis (1975) *The Haringey Rent Allowances Project – Second Interim Report,* Department of the Environment

A. Mackay (1974) *Social Indicators for Urban Sub-Areas: the Use of Administrative Records in the Paisley CDP,* Discussion Papers in Social research no. 5, University of Glasgow

L.D. McClements (1975) *Equivalence Scales for Children,* Department of Health and Social Security. Paper presented to the Conference on the Economics of Consumer Behaviour, 14-16 April 1975

D. Marsden (1973) *Mothers Alone: Poverty and the Fatherless Family,* Penguin

D. Marsden and E. Duff (1975) *Workless,* Penguin

R. Marshall (1972) *Families Receiving Supplementary Benefit: a Study comparing the Circumstances of some Fatherless Families and Familes of the Long-term Sick and Unemployed,* DHSS Statistical and Research Series no. 1, HMSO

A. Maynard (1972 unpublished) *Poverty in York – 1972 style,* University of York

Molly Meacher (1972) *Rate Rebates: a Study of the Effectiveness of Means Tests,* Child Poverty Action Group, Poverty research series 1

Ministry of Agriculture, Fisheries & Food (1974) *Household Food Consumption and Expenditure 1972,* HMSO

Ministry of Social Security (1967) *Circumstances of Families,* HMSO

National Community Development Project (1974) *Inter-Project Report 1973,* Centre for Environmental Studies

National Consumer Council (1975) *For Richer, for Poorer: Some Problems of Low-income Consumers*

D. Nevitt (1972) *Hidden Equalities and Family Income,* National Council for the Unmarried Mother and her Child

North Tyneside Community Development Project (1975) *The Impact of Income Maintenance Services: research outline*

Office of Population Censuses & Surveys (1975) *The General Household Survey 1972,* HMSO

D. Piachaud (1974) *Do the Poor Pay More?* Child Poverty Action Group

C. Pond (1975) 'Low wage-earners and the tax threshold', *Inflation and Low Incomes,* Fabian Research Series 322, Fabian Society

Preston Child Poverty Action Group (1972a) *Report on the Take Up of Family Income Supplement*

Preston Child Poverty Action Group (1972b) *Report on Poverty no. 2: Family Allowances*

R. Rooney and R. Woolf (1975) *Claimant to be Doubted? A Paper on Welfare Rights and the Homeless Single Person,* Grassmarket Urban Aid Project

B.S. Rowntree and G.R. Lavers (1951) *Poverty and the Welfare State*, Longmans

A. Sinfield (1970) 'Poor and out of work in Shields' in P. Townsend (ed.) *The Concept of Poverty*, Heinemann

A. Sinfield (1975) 'We the people and they the poor: a comparative review of poverty research' in *Social Studies: the Irish Journal of Sociology*, vol. 4:1

J. Streather and S. Weir (1974) *Single Mothers on Social Security*, Child Poverty Action Group, Poverty pamphlet 16

L. Syson (1975) 'Poverty in Camden: a report to the Department of Health and Social Security', *Clearing House for Local Authority Social Services Research* no. 12

L. Syson and M. Young (1974) 'Poverty in Bethnal Green', M. Young (ed.) *Poverty Report 1974*, Temple Smith

L. Syson and M. Young (1975) 'The Camden Survey', M. Young (ed.) *Poverty Report 1975*, Temple Smith

P. Townsend (1975) *Inflation and Low Incomes*, Fabian Research Series 322, Fabian Society

P. Townsend (forthcoming) *Poverty in the United Kingdom*

C. Trinder (1975) 'Changing Government Policies', M. Young (ed.) *Poverty Report 1975*, Temple Smith

Tunbridge Wells Child Poverty Action Group (1974) *Rent Allowances*

Tunbridge Wells Child Poverty Action Group (1975) *Report on Educational Benefits*

A. Walker (1975) 'Inflation and disabled people', *Inflation and Low Incomes*, Fabian Research Series 322, Fabian Society

York Child Poverty Action Group (1974) *Educational Welfare Benefits in York*

Index

Index